Praise for Other Books by Evelyn Jacks

Tax Secrets for Tough Times

To turn taxes into treasure, tax author and national treasure Evelyn Jacks has penned *Tax Secrets for Tough Times*. This is an essential guide for those faced with making critical decisions in times of personal crisis, but also for anyone who recognizes you can make and save money by learning more about tax planning.

Michael Kane, *The Vancouver Sun*

Make Sure It's Deductible, 2/e

Evelyn Jacks is well-deserving of her reputation as Canada's most trusted tax advisor. This book could save thousands of tax dollars for anyone who is self-employed, runs a small business, or is thinking of starting one.

Gordon Pape

The day you opened your small business is the day you stepped up to the plate to play ball with Canada Customs and Revenue Agency. In characteristic friendly style, Canada's foremost tax author lays out the rules of the game so that you and your family can minimize stress and maximize deductions. Prepare to be surprised and rewarded.

Michael Kane, *The Vancouver Sun*

Ms. Jacks draws on her expertise in a way that makes the argument for self-employment in this tax-oppressed country almost compelling.

Jonathan Chevreau, *The National Post*

For guidelines on the home office and all self-employment issues, I would recommend you read Evelyn Jacks' book *Make Sure It's Deductible* as a really good general and specific guide.

David Christianson, *Winnipeg Free Press*

Evelyn Jacks knows tax and writes about it in a way the average person can understand. That's a very unusual combination. Reading her advice will make you richer, especially if you deduct business expenses the way she tells you to in this book.

Ellen Roseman, *The Toronto Star*

Tax Savings
for the Long Run

How to Work with Your
TAX ADVISOR
for Maximum Gain

Tax Savings
for the Long Run

How to Work with Your
TAX ADVISOR
for Maximum Gain

Evelyn Jacks

McGraw-Hill
Ryerson

Toronto • Montréal • Boston • Burr Ridge, IL • Dubuque, IA • Madison, WI • New York
San Francisco • St. Louis • Bangkok • Bogotá • Caracas • Kuala Lumpur • Lisbon • London
Madrid • Mexico City • Milan • New Delhi • Santiago • Seoul • Singapore • Sydney • Taipei

ISBN 0-07-089453-1
1234567890 TRI 098765432

National Library of Canada Cataloguing in Publication

Jacks, Evelyn, 1955-
    Tax savings for the long run: how to work with your tax advisor for
    maximum gain / Evelyn Jacks.

Includes index.
ISBN 0-07-089453-1

1. Tax planning—Canada—Popular works. 2. Tax consultants—Canada. 3. Income tax—Canada—Popular works. I. Title.

HJ4661.J215 2002   343.7105'2   C2002-905141-1

Publisher: **Julia Woods**
Research Assistance: **Walter Harder & Associates**
Production Coordinator: **Andree Davis**
Editor: **Catherine Leek**
Electronic Page Design and Composition: **Heidy Lawrance Associates**
Cover Design: **Sharon Lucas**

Printed and bound in Canada

Table of Contents

What are your responsibilities as a tax filer? What are your taxpayer's rights? What are the consequences of tax avoidance and evasion? What responsibilities do professionals have? What transactions are subject to audit? How can you avoid penalties on errors or omissions? Strategize: Tips for analyzing and managing your responsibilities to CCRA.

Advisor Check-In 1.1: What to Do When You Get an Audit Letter

What are your objectives in retaining a professional? What are the benefits and limitations of each type of professional service? What should you expect to pay? How will you measure performance? How do you sever old relationships? How many advisors do you need? Strategize: Tips for analyzing your professional needs.

Advisor Check-In 2.1: Steps in Choosing a New Tax Advisor

Advisor Check-In 2.2: Interviewing a New Advisor

Chapter 6: Tax Strategies for Caregivers // 77

What is the tax filing profile of the advocate for the vulnerable? How can the burden of the sick and disabled by lightened from a tax point of view? How can their caregivers and advocates be empowered to take advantage of all the tax preferences available in these circumstances? Strategize: Tips for discussing a future of caregiving with your tax and financial advisors.

Advisor Check-In 6.1: Guide to Discussion About Child Care and Caregivers' Deductions

Advisor Check-In 6.2: Guide to Discussion About Non-Refundable Credits for Caregivers

Chapter 7: Tax Tips for Employees and Executives // 89

What are the key tax issues for employees? What are the most overlooked employment tax deductions and filing errors? What specific issues need to be considered if you work on a commission basis? Are there tax advantages to being self-employed? How can you turn job termination or lay-off into a tax advantage? Strategize: Discussion points for you and your advisor regarding the past, present and future of tax filing for employees.

Advisor Check-In 7.1: Questions to Ask About Employment Negotiations

Advisor Check-In 7.2: Employment-related Questions to Focus on Tax Savings

Chapter 8: Tips for Tax-Efficient Investing // 103

How can you take control of your family's legacy and the way you invest for the future? How much income will you need for retirement? How can tax planning help you withdraw funds more efficiently? How can new capital be generated from overpaid taxes of the past? How do you fund the lifestyle you want to live and preserve your capital tree? Strategize: Develop a plan with your advisor for the preservation of capital to live your retirement years without financial worry.

Advisor Check-In 8.1: Questions About Tax-Efficient Family Investment Planning

Advisor Check-In 8.2: Preparing to Discuss Investments with Your Advisor

Introduction

Do you suspect you're paying too much tax in spite of paying high fees for professional advice? How can you be certain that you are getting the best professional service possible? Do you feel you could be making better decisions about your financial future and your current tax and investment strategies?

You are among the millions of Canadians who turn their tax filing over to a professional each year. And, given the potential impact of tax planning on your personal wealth, paying for this professional expertise – whether a tax preparer or accountant, a financial planner, a lawyer, an investment counsellor or other financial services professional – may be one of the best investment decisions you have made.

But recruiting a strong advisor is only the first step. You then have to become a great coach, with a great game plan, to ensure that your advisor delivers the results you expect.

Tax Savings for the Long Run will show you how to take the management of your financial affairs to the next level. The main goal of this book is to give you the tools you need to become a great coach to your advisor. It will show you how, in conjunction with your tax professional, you can take control of your financial decision-making throughout the year and use Canadian tax law to build your wealth.

Specifically,

- You'll save time in pulling together your tax documents
- You'll save money on your current tax preparation fees
- You'll start making tax-wise decisions all year long to reduce the taxes you pay
- You'll be audit-proofed ... no more dreading the tax auditor, and
- You'll have the peace of mind that comes from knowing your advisor is doing what he or she was hired to do!

By reading this book, you will learn how to manage your professional relationships and bring the annual tax filing headache under control. You will learn about:

- **The Rules of Play:** Your obligations and those of your advisors in the tax compliance game
- **Talent Recruitment**: How to find a tax professional you can trust and who will meet your individual needs
- **Talent Replacement:** Tips on severing ties with your current professional if you find it's time for a change
- **Harvesting the Low Hanging Fruit:** Working with your advisor to recover overpaid tax or valuable provisions from past tax years
- **Game Plan Research:** A synopsis of the latest in tax news and how to use this information to your advantage when meeting with your advisor
- **Goal Setting and Plan Implementation:** New ways to add tax efficiency to your inter-generational investment decisions all year long
- **Organizing for Success:** A proven method for collecting and organizing relevant documentation to help your advisor prepare your family's taxes quickly and thoroughly
- **Plan Management:** Pertinent questions to ask your advisor to get the tax savings results you want
- **A Forward Focus:** Wise tax planning around changes in your career, business or education, or health care management within your family

To make this journey to tax-efficient wealth accumulation as easy as possible for you, this book is divided into three sections. The discussions in Chapters 1 to 5 provide easy-to-read guidelines surrounding the basic relationship and information exchange required between taxpayers and their financial advisors.

Chapters 6 to 10 zero in on the specific tax filing profiles most taxpayers fall into: caregivers, employees, investors, small business owners and executors, so that you can focus on ways to ensure that decisions you make throughout the year encompass the after-tax benefits our tax system provides especially for these profiles.

The final chapter in this book, At A Glance, provides 30 of the most commonly overlooked tax savings opportunities, to discuss with your advisors. Each tax provision will be described in three ways: what you need to know, what documents you need to bring and what questions you need to ask. We hope you find this chapter especially useful in isolating, with your advisors, every tax benefit you are entitled to. Skim through it not just once, but before every visit to your advisor or whenever there is a significant change in your personal or financial affairs.

At the end of each of the first ten chapters of the book, you'll also find two important features:

- **The Tax Pro Coach** — key communications strategies to strengthen the relationship with your advisors and coach them toward your desired results, so that they are better empowered to save you both time and money over the long run.
- **The Advisor Check-Ins** — practical details, checklists or topic-specific questions to facilitate the flow of the right information between you and your advisor.

These tools will help you to build a stronger relationship with your tax advisor. You will become an empowered taxpayer and the result can be a substantial increase in your personal wealth now and in the future.

CHAPTER 1

A Great Team Takes Responsibility

- Build a relationship of trust with your tax professional
- Know who's responsible for what
- Understand the consequences of errors and omissions
- Be prepared to handle an audit with your advisors

"Talk to my tax accountant ... he's in charge of the way my return was filed."

Sound familiar? Many people think that if they hire a tax professional to do their returns they are no longer responsible for how those returns are filed. Unfortunately, this is not the case. In fact, it is the taxpayer who is responsible for every figure on the tax return and accountable to Canada Customs and Revenue Agency (CCRA). If problems arise, you can't just absolve responsibility and blame tax audit woes on your tax preparer.

Because the onus of proof is on you, when you hire a professional, it is also your responsibility to be vigilant about your tax preparer's performance. But you have another equally important reason for managing this relationship with care. How you manage your tax affairs can significantly affect your tax savings over the long term. When you take all the taxes you pay into account (including liquor, amusement, excise, tobacco, auto taxes, payroll taxes, property taxes, income, sales and a variety of others), taxes are the biggest expense of your lifetime ... you will pay more in taxes than on food, clothing and shelter combined. However, income taxes which average 35% of the family's total tax bill, according to the Fraser Institute, are the only type of tax which allows some discretion. That is, you can arrange your affairs within the framework of the law to pay the least amount legally possible. Imagine shaving ten or 15% off that tax payable number on your return. If that number is $10,000 a year, you will have saved $400,000 over a productive lifetime of 40 years. That could be possible with proper tax planning and a great relationship with your tax advisory team.

You have hired a highly trained professional because you recognize this. Your responsibility now is to ensure that you are getting the best professional advice possible. For some, that's akin to critiquing a heart surgeon. How do you do it, if you don't have the knowledge or technical expertise? Fortunately, if you understand the basics, you can then work effectively with your advisor to control your taxes payable, establish your relationship with the tax department and maximize your tax savings over the long run.

MANAGING THE FIELD OF PLAY

It's next to impossible to be an expert at something you do only once a year. Despite this, filing your tax return is a manageable event and you can control the outcome — that's because you know how much money you made and where it is. You also know the circumstances of your career, business, family and investment affairs. Filing a tax return is simply the reconciliation of what happened in your personal and financial affairs last year.

There's no doubt about it: a taxpayer's obligation to file a correct return within the framework of the law can be onerous and, worse, the onus of proof is on you. It's no wonder that anxiety arises when organizing materials, communicating changes in your affairs and relying on someone else to keep your tax affairs onside. To do it well, and to your best advantage, it will pay to invest a bit of time to the process. The motivation? You'll become wealthier, your time will be better spent and you'll have less stress.

You really don't have to become a tax expert to take control of the taxes you pay or your responsibilities to comply. You simply need to have a great professional team to manage. You must, however, identify and recruit those team members according to your needs and empower them with the right information on a timely basis, so that they can do the best job possible for you. To be a great recruiter and establish a great working relationship with your tax team, you'll need to first understand the rules of the game and each party's obligation under them. This is discussed in the pages that follow. The recruitment of a new tax advisor is discussed in Chapter 2 and communicating effectively is discussed in Chapter 3.

WHAT ARE YOUR RESPONSIBILITIES?

You have a legal responsibility to CCRA (see Figure 1.1). Canadian residents are required to report *world income* in Canadian funds on their tax returns every calendar year (in the period January 1 to December 31). This includes not only income earned in cash, but also income received as bartered goods or services and income that is earned but not yet received.

Figure 1.1
Tax Filing Requirements

1. You must file a tax return every year to report your world income in Canadian funds.

2. Most Canadians must file a tax return by April 30 to avoid late filing penalties.

3. Unincorporated small business owners and their spouses can file by June 15, but interest will be charged after April 30 if there is a balance due.

4. You must report any offshore income, as well as the Canadian value of certain offshore holdings.

5. You must file to report the disposition of capital assets and to preserve loss carry-over applications.

6. You must file to receive your Old Age Security benefits, federal supplements to OAS and to contribute to the Canada Pension Plan if you are a proprietor.

7. You will want to file to claim refundable tax credits if you are income-eligible.

8. You will want to file to create unused Registered Retirement Savings Plan (RRSP) contribution room and carry forward unused deductions and credits like unused home office expenses, moving expenses, capital and non-capital losses, charitable donations and medical expenses.

9. You must file your taxes within the framework of the law so as to pay the least amount of taxes legally possible. If you circumvent the intent of the law, you may be participating in an avoidance transaction that may be ignored. If you participate in fraud — tax evasion — you can be fined and sent to jail. Tax evasion includes the understatement of income and the overstatement of expenses.

For the record, most Canadians are required to file a tax return by April 30, for the tax year ending December 31 the year before. However, those who report income or losses from an unincorporated small business may file their personal tax returns by June 15 without fearing a late filing penalty. However, this is not a good idea if you owe money to the tax department when you do file because interest will be charged from May 1 onward in those cases.

Many Canadians make their most critical error right at this juncture. First, they think to themselves, "Well, the government owes me money so no need to meet the tax filing deadline."

This is faulty logic. Why would you forego the ability to invest that money and earn income for your family or use it to pay down your non-deductible debts, like credit card bills or mortgage payments?

Further, by not filing or filing late, you may be compromising your position with CCRA for future claims under the Fairness Provisions (see later) and you could be missing important filing deadlines for specific provisions or missing carry-over opportunities for others.

Many people believe another myth. They think that if their money or assets are held offshore the Canadian government doesn't know about it and they don't have to report it. This is, of course, wrong. If your residency is here in Canada, you must report world income. Remember that Canada has tax treaties with over 60 countries, including agreements to share files with regard to your non-resident accounts.

Pay as Little Tax as Possible

It is your legal responsibility — to yourself and your family — to file a tax return every year within the framework of the law to pay the least amount of tax legally possible. Make sure you don't erode the productivity of your human and invested capital because of your tardiness in meeting your tax filing obligations by:

- avoiding filing penalties and interest costs
- using fast-filing methods to obtain your tax refunds as quickly as possible
- obtaining social benefits owed to you on time and in the right amounts
- preserving tax breaks you may be entitled to for use in future years
- preserving your options under the Fairness Package
- avoiding gross negligence and tax evasion penalties
- knowing your appeal rights when CCRA singles you out for audit.

Avoid Late Filing Penalties

If you have a balance due on April 30, filing late will result in a penalty of 5% of the unpaid amount plus 1% per month for a period of 12 months. Repeat offenders pay more if they fail to file on time again within a three year period: 10% of the unpaid amounts plus 2% per month for up to 20 months. In fact, for most tax filing delinquents, the interest and penalties can add up to be a much bigger problem than the taxes over a period of time. Interest compounds and accrues daily at a rate that is 4% higher than the rate paid on Canada Treasury Bills for the previous quarter.

If you find that you can't pay, file a return on time anyway to avoid the late filing penalties and possible gross negligence or tax evasion penalties. Then make arrangements to pay your bill, on time, if possible. Otherwise, you'll incur interest charges. However, this is still a better alternative than incurring both interest and penalty charges.

CCRA's interest clock ticks daily and on a compounding basis. It's better to know what you owe and then make other arrangements within your overall financial plan to deal with this reality. Owing CCRA is similar to owing a credit card balance, but with increased urgency ... wage garnishees, for example, are possible in extreme cases, as discussed later in this chapter. Deal with your tax bill first.

Get Your Refunds Quickly

When CCRA owes you money, you won't earn any interest on the amount until 45 days after the due date for the return or if you filed late, 45 days after the date you filed. The tax department tries to get the return processed before this deadline to save this expense.

Here's what this means to you: if you file two years late and the department owes you a refund of $3,000, you'll receive no interest on the overpayment if CCRA manages to process your tax return within 45 days of your filing date. Which begs the question: why give the tax department an interest free loan for all this time? File on time, get your money and use it to make more for yourself and your family.

Collect Social Benefits Owed to You

Even if you or your family members who are 18 or over have no taxable income for the year, it usually pays to file a tax return to receive refundable tax credits throughout the year. This includes two from the federal government: the Canada Child Tax Benefit (CCTB) and the Goods and Services Tax/Harmonized Sales Tax Credit (GST/HST Credit). There are also refundable tax credits available in some provinces. The statute of limitations for recovering these credits is shorter (it could be as little as 11 months, but CCRA does allow for some leniency when one spouse fails to file or in hardship cases), so filing on time is more important than ever.

Preserve Tax Breaks for Use in Other Tax Years

It is important to record capital and non-capital losses, unused RRSP contributions, moving expenses, unused home workspace expenses, unused capital cost allowances, charitable donations, medical expenses, tuition and education credits and student loan interest amounts. It is possible that some of these provisions may be applied back to recover refunds of taxes in the prior three years (this is the case for capital and non-capital losses) or carried forward to offset income in the future. Failing to file a return, therefore, has multi-year consequences.

Preserve Your Options Under the Fairness Package

Should you suffer a severe hardship in the future which causes you to file late (illness, death in the family, natural disasters, etc.), you may apply for leniency from the CCRA under its Fairness Package. The committee that reviews your request may grant you an extension for filing and/or waive penalties and interest. However it will take into account whether you have otherwise been a model tax filing citizen.

Avoid Gross Negligence and Tax Evasion Penalties

Procrastinators beware: don't push your luck with CCRA. If CCRA concludes that you are wilfully refusing to file a return, you may be hit with further penalties. Those who are found to be grossly negligent face additional penalties of 50% of the unpaid tax, plus the late filing penalty, plus the interest that continues to compound and accrue. Tax evaders face penalties of up to 200% of the unpaid tax, plus all the other penalties and interest and/or jail time. So, if you owe, bite the bullet and pay the tax — it's much cheaper than the alternative, a lot less stress and a better lifestyle option overall.

Know Your Appeal Rights when CCRA Singles You Out

Sometimes they are just wrong. Yes, CCRA does make mistakes and misinterprets your affairs. This is why you do have legal rights to challenge any tax assessment. But you must be careful to do it properly and on time. The general guidelines are as outlined.

- **Informal Objection.** When you perceive a mistake has been made in the initial assessment of your return, have your tax advisor write to CCRA to request an adjustment. If CCRA refuses to make the adjustment and you still believe they are incorrect, contact your tax professional immediately to discuss further options.
- **Objection-Income Tax Act (T400A).** This is a formal objection to the Chief of Appeals at the local Tax Services Office. It must be filed within one year after the taxpayer's filing due date or 90 days after the day of the mailing of the Notice of Assessment, whichever is later. You may indicate in this Notice that you wish to appeal directly to the Tax Court of Canada.
- **Appeals to the Tax Court of Canada.** An appeal may be made after the minister has confirmed the assessment or reassessment will stand or within 90 days after the service of an objection — if you did not receive a reply to the notice. This court has an informal procedure for federal taxes in dispute of $12,000 or less, under which you can represent yourself. It also has a general procedure which deals with amounts over this,

but requires the services of a lawyer. This court may dispose of the appeal by either dismissing it or allowing it in whole or part.
- **Appeals to Federal Court of Appeal.** If you have lost an appeal at the tax court level, informal procedures, you have 30 days from the date the decision was mailed to you or your representative to appeal to the Federal Court of Appeal. A lost case under the general procedure may be appealed to the Federal Court within 30 days from the date on which the judge signs the decision.
- **Appeals to the Supreme Court of Canada.** Appeals to the Supreme Court of Canada require the granting of permission to hear the appeal by the Supreme Court. The taxpayer has 60 days from the date of the judgment at the Federal Court of Appeal to file an application.

What are Your Rights as a Taxpayer?

As a taxpayer you have rights. In fact, they are enshrined in the Taxpayer's Declaration of Rights. In a nutshell, you have the right to:
- be presumed honest
- privacy and confidentiality
- an independent and impartial review if taxes are in dispute
- courtesy and consideration in all dealings with CCRA
- accurate and complete information about the Income Tax Act
- impartiality in the application of the law
- withhold taxes when amounts are in dispute
- bilingual services (French and English)
- every benefit under law: every Canadian tax filer is entitled to arrange affairs within the framework of the law to pay the least taxes legally possible.

There are many appeals and procedures you can take advantage of before CCRA will take drastic action on your delinquent file (see the section on Delinquency). Make sure you use those rights wisely.

What Are the Consequences of Delinquency?

You must pay your taxes and on time. You have learned that if you don't pay on time, you'll be charged interest and penalties. If you are negligent in keeping records or preparing your return or turn a blind eye to the way your tax return was done, you'll pay a gross negligence penalty. And if you wilfully defraud the government — understate your income or overstate deductions or claim refundable tax credits under fraudulent information — you'll be charged with tax evasion.

And CCRA will be quite persistent.

- **They can Refuse to Accept Your Return as Filed.** Yes, it's true. The minister can redo your return — his way — under the following powers:
  - Section 152(7) gives CCRA the power *not to accept your tax return as filed* and may make its own assessment of the amount of tax it believes you should pay.
  - Section 152(8) makes the assumption that CCRA is correct in its assessments, *unless those assessments are challenged by the taxpayer.*

  It is therefore important for all taxpayers to understand that they, not CCRA, bear the burden of proof. But, the onus is also on you to fight for your legal rights. So the worst thing you can do when your tax return is reassessed is nothing.

  Also know that, if CCRA alleges fraud, the burden shifts to the tax department to prove that there was intent to defraud the government and commit a crime. It is your right to put the government to strict proof of this issue.

- **They can Withhold Your Tax Refund.** CCRA can use your current year's tax refund to offset taxes you owe in a prior year or, if you are delinquent in making child support payments, your refund can be reallocated to your ex-spouse for those purposes. So be sure you stay current with your obligations. But if you aren't, don't commit your refund for other purposes. There are close to 50 other government departments that can lay claim to your tax refunds including the following:
  - *Federal:* Agriculture and Agri-Food Canada, Atlantic Canada Opportunities Agency, Canada Economic Development, Canada Mortgage and Housing Corporation, Canada Transport Agency, Citizen and Immigration Canada, Fisheries and Oceans Canada, Human Resources Development Canada, Industries Canada, Justice Canada, National Defence, Public Works Canada, Statistics Canada, Western Economic Diversification Canada.
  - *Provincial:* Various departments dealing with student loans and social assistance overpayments.
- **They can Garnish Your Wages.** This can be quite embarrassing, so never ignore requests for information from CCRA. Know, however that the CCRA can't garnish your wages for taxes owing if taxes are in dispute, that is, if you have begun an appeals process. Therefore it always pays to file a formal Objection promptly if you disagree with your assessment or reassessment. This will also preserve your appeal rights in the future. Talk to your tax advisor about this.
- **They can Show up at Your Door.** If you get an unexpected visit from a CCRA tax auditor, be polite and courteous, but ask for a letter outlining

what information they require and by when. Then consult your tax advisor. If they show up with a summons, consult your tax advisor and a lawyer immediately.

- **They can Charge Penalties and Interest.** Take a moment now to familiarize yourself with the financial consequences of tax delinquency (see Figure 1.2) — not a good addition to your overall financial plan.

Figure 1.2
Top Tax Penalties Chargeable by CCRA

Circumstance	Penalty
Failure to file a return on time	5% of unpaid taxes plus 1% per month up to a maximum of 12 months from filing due date, which is June 15 for unincorporated small businesses
Subsequent failure to file on time within a 3-year period	10% of unpaid taxes plus 2% per month to a maximum of 20 months from filing due date
Failure to provide information on a required form	$100 for each failure
Failure to provide Social Insurance Number	$100 for each failure unless the card is applied for within 15 days of the request
Failure to provide information with regard to foreign-held property	$500 per month for a maximum of 24 months; $1,000 a month for a maximum of 24 months if there is a failure to respond to a demand to file plus an additional penalty of 5% of the value of the property transferred or loaned to a foreign trust or the cost of the foreign property where failure to file exceeds 24 months
Gross negligence: false statement or omission of information in the return	50% of tax on understated income with a minimum $100 penalty
False statements or omissions with regard to foreign properties	5% of the value of the property, minimum of $24,000
Late or insufficient instalments	50% of interest payable exceeding $1,000 or 25% of interest payable if no instalments were made, whichever is greater
Tax Evasion	50% to 200% of tax sought to be evaded and imprisonment for up to 5 years
Failure to deduct or remit source deductions	10% of amount not withheld, or remitted
Second such failure in same year	20% of amount not withheld or remitted if this was done knowingly or through gross negligence

Tax Query
What Transactions Are Subject to Audit?

Generally speaking Canadian taxpayers are governed by a system of self-assessment. That means you voluntarily comply with the law to report income and deductions and credits. CCRA can then check to see if your reporting is accurate and follow the law by conducting an audit. The following entries on your return are at greater risk of audit than others:

- Income: Any income that is not reported on a T Slip: self-employment, rental income, support payments, etc.
- Deductions: RRSP, child care expenses, attendant care expenses, business investment losses, moving expenses, support payments made, carrying charges and interest expenses, employment expenses, other deductions.
- Non-Refundable Tax Credits: Disability amounts, interest paid on student loans, tuition and education amounts, medical expenses and charitable donations.
- Refundable Tax Credits: Child tax benefits and certain provincial tax benefits

If you are claiming any of these on your tax return, be sure that you and your tax advisor have reviewed all receipts carefully before making the claims and can easily justify the figures in case of audit. Then file the information in a safe place because the likelihood if needing to retrieve them in the near future is high.

How Can You Avoid Penalties on Errors and Omissions?

It is possible to avoid penalties when you discover an error or omission. Under CCRA's Fairness Package, taxpayers who come forward to correct errors and omissions may do so without penalty. Interest will be charged and taxes must be paid on a timely basis. However, if taxes cannot be paid at once, the tax department will arrange for instalment tax payments to be made on a reasonable basis.

Ask your tax advisor about correcting errors and omissions on your return if you become aware that you have missed claiming an income, deduction or credit provision or if you find receipts for provisions you could have claimed but didn't.

WHAT ARE THE RESPONSIBILITIES OF YOUR TAX PROFESSIONAL?

Tax professionals have responsibilities to you to prepare your return accurately, based on the information you have provided to them. It is general practice to require you to sign a disclaimer absolving them of responsibility if you do not provide all the information or if you provide false information. You should always inquire about the guarantees of service if the tax pro makes a mistake.

You should also know that there are civil penalties your tax pro can be charged with if he participates in fraud or counsels you in fraud. According to the law, your tax and financial advisors can be held liable for:

Culpable conduct in cases occurring after June 29, 2000 if their conduct is:
- intentional in the commitment of fraud and/or the fraudulent participation in planning or valuation activities that lead to reduction, avoidance or deferral of taxes
- indifferent as to whether they are complying with their obligations under the Income Tax Act
- wilful, reckless or wanton in their disregard for the law.

Financial planners who act as tax advisors can also be implicated if they show culpable conduct. This includes activities that cause a subordinate to act in a manner that displays culpable conduct or to omit information or to do nothing to prevent the participation of a subordinate to omit information or act in a culpable way. It must be shown that the advisor made a reasonable attempt to prevent such activities.

So, if you fall victim to an unscrupulous planner, be heartened by the fact that both of you have consequences under the law. Those consequences, for participants in culpable conduct, include fines starting at a minimum of $1,000.

Beyond the Legal Responsibilities

Your relationship with a tax advisor is most important to your overall lifetime financial results. Don't take this lightly or make the mistake of curbing your expense budget here. When you hire a highly trained professional, you have every right to expect more from him than the responsibilities outlined above. Your tax pro should also be willing to communicate clearly and fully in order to advise you on the best course of action to ensure your tax affairs are handled most effectively over the long run. Your brother-in-law may be able to prepare your tax return for free, but remember it is the long-term results of your well-informed, year-round decision making that are important. This is the key advantage of paying professional dollars.

Therefore, if you have made the decision to seek a tax professional, or change to a new one, you need to feel comfortable asking all kinds of questions about how your tax rights and obligations relate to the circumstances of your life. You need to be able to check up on the accuracy of your tax filing process by asking intelligent questions and you have the right to expect that you will receive well-researched, well-communicated answers back from your advisor. You need someone who is willing to educate you.

If you are uneasy about any aspect of your tax filing affairs or are not communicating well with your tax pro, get a second opinion.

TAX PRO COACH
Your Strategic Plan to Meet Your Tax Filing Obligations
To build a strong relationship with your advisory team, you have to know the rules and insist that they be followed to your best legal advantage. Ensure these concepts are clear to you:

- Do I understand my basic obligations and responsibilities under the Income Tax Act?
- Do I understand my taxpayer rights?
- Do I understand what provisions on my returns are most likely to be audited this year?
- Do I understand what the penalties are when I file offside?
- How can I be proactive about errors or omissions and circumvent penalties?
- Who do I call if the tax department arrives or requests a tax audit?
- What are the responsibilities of my professional tax advisor, under law and to me?
- Do I understand how my tax advisor will take responsibility for his errors or omissions?

Knowing your rights and obligations, and how to handle errors and omissions will help you go forward with peace of mind and confidence in arranging your affairs within the framework of the law.

Advisor Check-In 1.1
What to Do When You Get an Audit Letter

A great relationship with your tax advisor really pays off during a tax audit. How can you interact most effectively with your tax pro to ensure your own peace of mind and the best outcomes?

- **Act Immediately.** Go to see that tax advisor, immediately, with all the records you can find for the tax years being audited. If you did your tax returns yourself, now is the time to hire a professional. Read Chapter 2.
- **Set Aside Time to Work with Your Tax Advisor.** You'll need to work with your advisor to put together the appeal. To win and save yourself a significant amount of money, a tax audit will require your personal resources of time.
- **Be Prepared to Go Back and Look through Old Files.** Your advisor will likely ask you to go back and recover duplicate receipts, create auto logs from the information in your daily business journal, etc.
- **Anticipate Your Outcomes.** Together with your tax advisor, quantify your upside and your down-side. Your upside would be one of two things:
  - no changes are made to the return
  - you uncover a tax filing method, provision or new receipts that have been previously missed and use these to have your taxes decreased for the year.

  Your downside could be one of three things:
  - taxes are increased because source documents for write-offs are missing
  - taxes are increased because tax losses are disallowed
  - taxes are increased because income reported is adjusted upward.
- **Rely on Your Advisor.** Your advisor will take care of many tasks.
  - He'll make sure the deadlines are met. The response to the audit letter is the first milestone; filing an Objection is the second.
  - He'll request extensions. CCRA as a rule will grant an extension from their normal turn-around time of 30 days, under reasonable circumstances.
  - He'll review your documents, logbooks and other records and identify any problem areas in your position.
  - He'll review CCRA's claims and identify any problems in their position.
  - He'll review the new provisions for the year being audited and ensure all new deductions and credits were noted.

CHAPTER 2

Defining Your Need for a Tax Advisor

■ Define your goals in hiring a tax professional
■ Know what services a tax professional can provide
■ Determine the cost and what services you are paying for
■ Measure your advisor's performance

Have you ever left a tax preparer's office feeling frustrated that you just paid a large sum of money for something that you didn't fully understand, but were ultimately responsible for? Or did you wonder if you had really received the best advice possible? Many people just don't get the results they want from their tax advisor.

Some people have a similar experience as they leave an appointment with their family doctor, after learning of a diagnosis of a serious illness. They are thrust into a world of unfamiliar medical terms, procedures and therapies and faced with the responsibility of making life-altering decisions regarding treatment.

Fortunately, you don't have to know how to do a heart by-pass to understand the treatment and how the operation will affect you and your family. Your doctor has an obligation to communicate the effects and outcomes of this operation so that you can cope with the results.

Likewise, you don't need to be able to do a tax return to ensure you have, in fact, claimed all the deductions and credits you are entitled to. However, you do need to be conversant in the language of the business in order to get the results you want. We'll help you with this in Chapter 3, but first, you must find the advisor that's right for you, one who can help you achieve control and peace of mind in filing your annual tax return while planning ahead to minimize the taxes you pay in the future.

This begins by defining — or redefining — your needs.

WHY DO YOU NEED A TAX PROFESSIONAL?

Most Canadians have the ability to do their own tax returns. Tax preparation is a life skill that is taught in many high schools. But, for many reasons roughly half of Canadian tax filers turn to someone else to prepare their tax returns for them every year. Perhaps you don't want to commit the considerable time it takes to do your own or your family's returns. Perhaps your financial affairs are becoming more complex with growing income, investments and expenses. Or you may have a growing small business or home business that merits the attention of a tax professional. Or perhaps you just have that nagging feeling that you may be overlooking potential tax deductions or opportunities to manage your tax planning in a more beneficial way.

There are dozens of ways that an advisor can help you as shown in Figure 2.1 But, in general, there are ten reasons why tax filers turn to a tax professional.

1. Something new happens in your personal affairs.
2. You are being audited.
3. You simply don't have time to do the return.
4. You are not confident it's right — it is difficult to excel at something you only do once a year.
5. You don't have the time to research tax news or learn how to use tax software.
6. You don't understand tax jargon.
7. There is usually more than one way to prepare a tax return mathematically correctly and you want it done to your best benefit.
8. You want to make better decisions about your tax savings opportunities all year long.
9. You need someone to help you match the continuous changes in income tax law and policy, on a federal and provincial basis, with the changes in your personal situation.
10. You want peace of mind and assurance you are meeting your responsibilities under the law.

A closer look at the top two reasons for turning to a tax professional may provide some insight into your own needs.

Figure 2.1

How and When a Tax Pro Can Help

In General

- I don't have time to prepare my own tax return
- I failed to file a tax return sometime in the past
- I need to submit an amendment to a prior-filed return
- I am being audited

When Personal Relationships Change

- I'm getting married or divorced
- I'm changing the terms of a separation agreement
- I'm starting to live in a conjugal relationship
- I'm expecting a child or grandchild
- I make significant charitable donations
- I'm thinking of setting up a trust
- I'm moving out of my home town or home province
- I'm buying or selling cottages or other vacation properties
- Someone in my family is ill
- Someone in my family is entering a nursing home
- There is a death in my family
- I'm thinking of giving money or transferring assets to my spouse, common-law partner or minor child or grandchild
- I'm inheriting money or assets

When Career or Business Circumstances Change

- Before I start a new job
- I'm starting a job in which I'm expected to pay my own expenses
- I'm using my car or home for both personal and employment or business purposes
- I'm having a spouse or child work for me
- I'm not sure if I'm employed or self-employed
- I started or am thinking of starting a business
- I'm thinking of incorporating a business
- I'm buying new assets: computers, furniture, a building
- I haven't kept track of the values of assets I have acquired over the years
- I'm closing or thinking of closing a business
- I have a business in another country or another province

When Income Changes

- I receive lump sums of any kind, including a signing bonus, severance
- I receive income from commissions
- My employer provides me with a vehicle, educational opportunities, other perks
- I'm using frequent flyer points earned in employment or business for personal use
- I'm using goods purchased in my business for personal consumption
- I make tips
- I receive income from wage loss replacement plans
- I trade in securities or real estate
- I have rental properties
- I own a farm
- I have income from a foreign country
- I hold property offshore with a total cost of more than $100,000 (Cdn)
- I have non-resident dependants
- I have a rental property in a foreign country

With Expenditures

- I have medical expenses, charitable donations or political contributions
- I'm going to post-secondary school or support someone who does
- I support children, parents, grandparents or other dependants
- I think I have under- or over-contributed to my RRSP
- I want to borrow money to invest in the stock market
- I need money to buy a home or go back to school
- I have unusual transactions surrounding my company pension plan
- I have auto expenses
- Before I buy or lease a car
- I have home office expenses
- I need to keep track of the expenses of a small business
- Before I buy or lease assets that will be used in my business
- I'm hiring sub-contractors; I'm hiring family members
- I'm thinking of borrowing money to make purchases of any kind

When Something New Happens in Your Life

In 1997 Ernst & Young prepared a survey for *The Globe and Mail* which revealed that about 1% of Canadians were millionaires. This number was expected to triple by 2005. It was interesting to read about how Canadian millionaires were created. Most came upon their good fortune through inheritances. Others became wealthy through the sale of their assets, in particular their small business corporations. Of all the millionaires surveyed, 43% had been investing their wealth in interest-producing savings; 57% had used products like mutual funds and shares.

Since that time, there has been significant change in the world, which has trickled down to everyday life. The stock markets have fluctuated with volatility, certain industry sectors have been hit with layoffs or closures and many Canadians have decided to retire from their jobs to begin small businesses of their own. Others have endured personal misfortune: a family member has become ill, there has been a separation or divorce or care is being given to mom or dad, grandpa or grandma. Yet others have benefited from an unexpected windfall: an inheritance, a quick profit in the stock market, a scholarship for their university-bound child. It is during times of change that people stand to gain the most from paying attention to their tax affairs. This is when you should be asking tax questions and seeking help.

Will your family be among those who become new millionaires in the next several years? It is very possible if you take a tax-first view to your productivity. Will the changes in your life — happy or sad — that bring lump sums of money to your door translate to significant and well-managed after-tax reserves? If you don't know, a qualified tax advisor can help.

When You're Being Audited

For most people, a tax audit is a scary proposition and a time when they turn to a tax professional. Although every tax filer must be prepared for this eventuality, a tax audit is more likely for those who are self-employed and for those who claim deductions that are receipt-based, such as the following:

- child care expenses
- moving expenses
- investment carrying costs
- expenses of self-employment
- employment expenses, especially if commission sales based
- extensive medical expenses or charitable donations
- any GST/HST-based claims, particularly if the government owes you money.

A tax audit is best handled by a qualified third party. It is, after all, an intensely emotional affair for even the most competent and confident taxpayer. In your quest for the right tax advisor, therefore, you are also looking for someone who will be a skilful representative before CCRA.

Tax Query
How can a Tax Pro Help Meet Your Objectives?

- By preparing your taxes accurately and on time, in an audit-proofed fashion.
- By preparing your tax returns to the family unit's best benefit over a period of years.
- By assisting you in making tax-efficient investment decisions.
- By helping you to exercise your legal right to make tax-wise decisions throughout the year (not just at tax time).
- By helping you to provide wealth for next generations with intelligent estate planning.
- By ensuring that your files are audit-proof.

WHAT SERVICES CAN A TAX PROFESSIONAL PROVIDE?

In discussing the services of a tax professional, we are making an important assumption: that you are seeking the services of a highly qualified person, who has either the appropriate post-secondary degree or certification, as required, and that her continuing education in tax updating has been recent. It is appropriate to enquire about qualifications of both your accountant and the people who work on your return behind the scenes.

There are many kinds of tax services performed by qualified professionals. The most common ones are: commercial tax services like storefronts or mall kiosks managed individually or by national or international tax preparation firms, accountants, lawyers, financial planners and other financial companies. The services of a different type of tax pro may be appropriate at different times in your tax filing lifetime, depending upon your personal needs. They can include tax preparation, tax planning, assistance with tax audits, electronic filing or tax discounting, a service in which the tax return is prepared and the refund is provided to the tax payer immediately in return for a legislated percentage. Some companies will even check your self-prepared return for a fee. Inquire about the variety of services your potential tax professional can offer you.

Who is Best to Fill Your Needs?

With so many advisors offering the same services, how do you decide who is best for you? It's not easy and your decision may depend as much on your personal comfort level with the individual as their formal training. Following are some general guidelines for the most common professional services available.

When to Consult an Independant Tax Preparer

At tax time there are many independant tax preparers offering services on a seasonal basis. This may be a solution if your tax affairs are extremely simple (credit filers, simple employment or investment profiles) and expected to stay that way in the foreseeable future. These independants can often prepare tax returns at a lower cost because they don't bear the burden of year-round operating costs. Be sure that the preparer can demonstrate she has taken an updating tax course and inquire about guarantees of service, how to reach the person in the off-season and whether the fees include copies of the return and audit-assistance at no extra cost. An independant may also have a professional designation and a well-developed long-term clientele. Ask for referrals to other clients to assess their satisfaction levels. An independant tax preparer can generally:

- prepare simple personal tax returns
- help adjust a prior-filed tax return
- may provide copies of returns
- may provide some electronic filing services
- may provide year-round services
- may provide a guarantee of service
- may provide audit assistance.

When to Consult a Commercial Tax Preparer

Under the proviso that you find a commercial preparation company which is available all year to provide audit assistance should your return be questioned by CCRA , and which guarantees the work, a commercial tax services company is the right professional to consult for tax preparation work. Commercial tax companies do more returns than most accountants or financial planners and can provide services at a reasonable fee. Consider using a commercial service even when you are using another professional for more complicated tax matters (corporate, trust or estate planning) or financial planning. A commercial service will :

- prepare simple personal tax returns for you or family members
- provide electronic filing services
- double-check your self-prepared tax return
- help adjust a prior-filed tax return
- handle simple audit requests from CCRA
- provide year-round assistance
- provide copies of returns
- provide a guarantee of service.

When to Consult an Accountant

Having your personal tax returns prepared by an accountant can be expensive, so you'll want to interview prospective accountants with care. In general, however, you should consider an accountant in the following scenarios:

- when you want books and tax returns done for a small business — but ask for an estimate and/or a referral to a competent, but affordable bookkeeper
- when you need GST/HST and PST filing assistance
- when you need assistance transferring your assets from a proprietorship to a corporation
- when you are setting up a family trust or an estate freeze
- to prepare a corporate tax return
- to prepare trust returns
- buying or selling businesses or issuing shares
- creation or dissolution of partnerships, including husband/wife partnerships
- to set up relationships with lawyers relating to inter-family investment transactions, to draw up a family trust or to assist with estate planning, business structure, prenuptial agreements, etc.
- to prepare a final return upon emigration or death of a taxpayer
- to provide assistance with offshore holdings.

When to Consult a Financial Planner

Unlike commercial tax preparers and accountants whose services are often historical in nature or lawyers who operate in the present to deal with past events or future outcomes, the financial planner's mandate is to help you plan for your future and your family's, providing a process for defining your life and after-life goals. This may include:

- a formal financial plan, outlining your goals, risk tolerance and time horizons for wealth creation
- management assistance in all financial transactions, acquisitions and dispositions
- assistance with certain financial transactions only: accumulating investments based on your individual investment goals, creating income, assistance in managing inter-generational wealth
- to do the above in the most tax-effective basis.

A Year-Round Commitment

Many people think that their income tax filing worries end on April 30, but as far as the tax department is concerned, this is only the beginning of the process. It is important to understand that Canada Customs and Revenue

Agency (CCRA) can and will seek more information about your filing, request more money or require your presence in front of a tax auditor. For these reasons, it is important that your tax preparer be available all year.

KEY CHARACTERISTICS OF THE BEST ADVISORS

After you have identified what services you need and which qualified tax professional is best trained to meet your needs, you should consider the softer skills that are so necessary.

It is important to work with an individual tax preparer who wishes to establish a long-term relationship with you. The annual task of tax preparation can then move towards a more desirable, results-focused goal: tax planning throughout the year. Your professional should have the following personal qualities:

- great integrity and professionalism to ensure that your confidentiality is preserved
- desire and ability to communicate well
- curiosity to dig for new provisions that can save you money
- ability to meet deadlines and deal with stress
- strong communication skills to answer your questions and explain the more complicated tax issues in easy-to-understand language.

Strong Peripheral Vision

You want a tax pro who will be vigilant about continuously reviewing your prior-year tax returns. You may have forgotten to mention something that makes a difference in the past, present or future. Those prior-filed returns can be amended for most federal provisions, all the way back to 1985, and for most provincial provisions, for the current year and the previous two years. Expect changes in these time limits in the future, as provinces grapple with mistakes or adjustments required under the new TONI tax calculations.

A Great Teacher

You also want to work with a tax pro who is an educator. You should feel comfortable asking questions relating to your current tax affairs, the affairs of your family members, the tax consequences of your up-coming financial decisions and your concerns about inter-generational tax planning. If your tax advisor is not interested in spending the time with you, is uncommunicative or just takes your information and hands it back to you with a bill, it's time to look for another advisor.

An Eye to the Future

You need to take the time to understand how much tax you pay today, what you could have done to reduce your tax liability last year and what you can do in the future to pay less tax. What income tax bracket do you fall into and how are your various income sources taxed? What is your marginal tax rate? How do you split off income to your spouse or children? You especially need a clear understanding of any carry-forward figures and how they will be applied in the future to reduce your taxes payable.

There is another reason this information is critical: you must communicate it to your executors, as described in Chapter 10. There are important tax savings opportunities in the event of death that stem from historical tax data. Ask for it and keep it in a safe place.

You are now ready to find the advisor who is right for you. Advisor Check-In 2.1 outlines the steps to follow in making that decision. It is a good idea to interview three different professionals, for example, an independent preparer, a commercial tax preparation firm and an accountant, to give you a sense of the types of services, prices and follow-up available. Before walking into that initial interview, consider what questions you will ask. Advisor Check-In 2.2 offers suggested questions that can help you to evaluate whether you've found the right advisor for you.

HOW MUCH SHOULD YOU PAY FOR TAX PREPARATION?

While many of us could fix a car, sew a dress or draft a legal agreement, we often choose to buy these services instead because the time saved and the peace of mind received is worth more to us than the money we pay to buy it. It's also nice to know that an expert who does nothing but this type of work is applying skill and experience to our needs. Paying for tax preparation falls under the same rationale.

Many pay for tax services reluctantly — undervaluing the work and paying little attention to the results. These tax filers are likely not interested in ongoing tax planning assistance. If all you want is data entry and tax calculation, your fees should be lowest.

Others are interested in paying for a higher level of service and require higher knowledge and experience levels. Many taxpayers, especially professionals like doctors, lawyers or small business owners, are reluctant to ask about the cost of those tax preparation services. Often they are shocked by the size of their professional's bill and do not understand the services that are included in the fee. Don't hesitate to ask: it is definitely appropriate to ask your professional a series of questions about the fees for services being offered.

Tax Query
What Questions should I ask about Professional Tax Preparation Fees?

- What the tax preparation fees will be?
- What services are included: for example, is there year-round service at no extra cost?
- What happens if there are errors or omissions on the return?
- Will the tax professional stand behind the work: are there guarantees?
- Are fees refunded and/or interest and penalty costs reimbursed when an error is the preparer's fault?
- Will the professional represent you during a tax audit?

Tax preparation fees can vary from under $100 for the simplest returns to several thousands of dollars for personal and corporate return preparation. How well your records are presented will have a bearing on this fee. That's why it's important to be organized.

If you are a busy executive, entrepreneur or caregiver who should be out there making money or otherwise doing something more important than inching through the crawl space for receipts or keeping bookkeeping journals: delegate. Make sure you have an assistant who takes control of the documentation all year, whether that's your spouse or someone you hire for that purpose. Time is money and filing your return under pressure with half your documentation missing due to your disorganization is simply too expensive in the long run.

Be prepared to invest either your own time or some of your money in bookkeeping throughout the year. It makes no sense to leave an entire year's bookkeeping activities to April 30. This is a sure-fire way to miss deductions you are entitled to.

See Chapter 4 to learn more about presenting your information in a manner which can save you time and money in your professional fees. Even if you're a hopeless bookkeeper, this method of document gathering can still work for you.

EVALUATE YOUR ADVISOR'S PERFORMANCE

Once you have established a relationship with a tax advisor, it is important to have a series of performance markers in place to review your relationship and its effectiveness and empower you and your advisors to meet your long-term tax savings goals. To ensure this, you must make the following tax queries:

- Was the return filed on time?
- Did CCRA agree with the way the return was filed?
- If there was a discrepancy, who was at fault — CCRA or the tax professional?
- Did you provide all the information to accurately complete the return? If not, did your pro ask you about the provision?
- Is your tax pro up-to-date with her tax knowledge? Can she readily answer questions about tax news or upcoming changes in federal or provincial tax law?
- Does your tax pro review prior-filed returns for carry-forward information or provisions that may have been missed?
- Does your tax pro review the taxes you pay all year by analyzing your tax withholding at source or the amount of your quarterly instalment payments?
- Does your tax pro do "what if" scenarios: what if your income sources were diversified, what if you contributed more to an RRSP, what if you split income with family members?
- Is your tax pro willing to meet with you throughout the year to answer your questions about the tax consequences of personal or financial decisions you are contemplating?
- Does your tax pro have the ability and confidence to defend your filings in case of audit?
- Can your tax pro work with other financial planning professionals or your lawyer to ensure your complete tax and financial planning objectives are met?

If the majority of the answers to the questions above are "no," you should consider making a change. You may have outgrown your tax pro.

HOW DO YOU SEVER OLD RELATIONSHIPS?

Sometimes long-term relationships become stagnant or your circumstances change to such a degree that a new approach or skill level is required from your tax advisors. If this is so in your situation, it can leave you feeling very uncomfortable severing a relationship.

Often taxpayers wait for something to go wrong — sometimes repeatedly — before they make this decision. It is less uncomfortable for them to deal with the errors or the potential for error than the reality of making the change.

However, for all these reasons it is important for you to take control because the old relationship could be costing you lots of money now or in the future. Your tax advisor — if she is a true professional — would not want this to happen, either. You can take a couple approaches to severing ties.

Speak with your current advisor, asking for a referral to a new professional when new skill sets are required. For example, if your commercial tax preparer does not have the skills to help you incorporate your growing proprietorship, set up a family trust or a new partnership, buy or sell assets, etc., it is entirely appropriate to ask for a referral. Use the opportunity to thank your pro for an excellent relationship to date.

Seek out a new professional and ask that your files be transferred. In this way, you need not deal with the matter yourself, however, it still may be a good idea to communicate either a special thank you or the reasons why you have decided to seek a new relationship. If your former tax pro is concerned about her business, you will likely receive a phone call asking for this feedback at any rate.

HOW MANY ADVISORS DO YOU NEED?

You may find that you need the services of several professional advisors. For example, you may require the services of a financial advisor throughout the year to help you with your investment transactions, a lawyer to help with the updating of your will and a tax pro well-versed in the tax consequences of those transactions. If your financial planner otherwise does a good job, but is not necessarily a tax expert, ensure that you bring into your professional advisory circle someone who is. This can be on referral of your financial planner or an unrelated third party who may give you a different approach to your financial affairs. Under no circumstances should taxes be dealt with completely separately from other financial advice you receive throughout the year.

Remember, the quality of your tax planning is a joint responsibility. When you decide to seek out a new tax advisor, be prepared to work at becoming a great coach to help your advisor meet your objectives. Read the tips in the Tax Pro Coach following, but also keep in mind that to have a rewarding relationship with your tax pro you must provide her with quality information. To do this effectively, however, you'll need a starter kit of general tax knowledge, the subject of Chapter 3.

TAX PRO COACH
Your Strategic Plan to Define Your Needs for a Tax Advisor
Deciding whether you need a tax advisor is the first step. Selecting the advisor that fits your needs and can work with you to provide on-going advice is paramount to your tax planning future. Consider the following questions and issues regarding your relationship with your tax pro:

- Re-evaluate whether my relationship with my current advisor is working. Is she providing me with the services I require? Am I able to make informed financial decisions throughout the year?
- Are the costs of using a tax professional's services offset by the benefits I receive?
- Review how many times a year I want to meet with my tax professional. Is she willing to meet with me more than during tax preparation season? Can she offer me advice beyond strictly completing my return?
- Determine whether I require more than one professional advisor and, if so, whether it is possible to get them to work together. Will they all meet with me at once to create a game plan?

Advisor Check-In 2.1
Steps in Choosing a New Tax Advisor

As this is a long-term relationship, often as significant as the relationship you have with your doctor, take time in the selection process.

Seek Referrals. Ask friends and business associates for referrals; check out the yellow pages and Chamber of Commerce or Board of Trade in your area for the names of well-respected tax advisors.

Expertise and Services Needed. Determine what level of expertise you need: commercial tax prepara-tion, accounting and auditing, corporate as well as personal returns, trust returns and estate plan-ning. See What Services Can a Tax Professional Provide.

Reputation and Experience. Interview at least three professionals in your area. This can include inde-pendants, partners in a partnership, large commercial firms, and so on. It's best to include one from every group to get the best overview of potential service, quality and price. You will receive a broad sampling of services and fees and, most important, an opportunity to judge the effectiveness of communications with you.

Ask Questions. Come to the interview prepared to ask about your top three taxation concerns. (See Advisor Check-In 2.2.)

Listen Well. When you ask your questions, take note of the way the answers are communicated to you. Can you learn from this person? Is the person willing to help you learn? Is the person interested in you and your business? Does she make suggestions to you? Does she have a strong background in taxation? The last thing you need is to feel intimidated or unclear about the way your concerns were addressed. You are looking for peace of mind and a professional partner for the future of your business and personal affairs.

Find Out About Service. Ask about fee structure. Can you be provided with fee estimates? What is the guarantee of service provided? Does the professional have errors or omissions insurance and what will she take responsibility for when errors occur? Who pays for interest and penalties assessed by CCRA in case of error? What is the size of the organization and what additional services can be provided? Do the services include double-checking of the preparation work, a review of previously filed returns, year-round consulting services, photocopying services, will you receive a copy of the full return or only a summary, do the fees include electronic filing services?

Integrated Services. Ask about the professional's ability to interact with others: lawyers, financial plan-ners, insurance advisors and so on, should you need these services.

Make the Decision. Choose the advisor you are most comfortable with.

Give a Trial. Ask the advisor to complete a small job to see if there is integrity behind the quality of the work, the ability to meet deadlines and to work with you on follow-up procedures.

Review the Accuracy of the Work. Listen and learn as the advisor explains the results of the work to you. If she is not interested in explaining, it's time to move on.

Advisor Check-In 2.2
Interviewing a New Advisor

Use the questions below to guide you through an initial interview with a tax advisor. Take them with you into the interview and don't forget to write down the answers you receive.

1. I have three major concerns about my tax affairs. They are:

1. _____

2. _____

3. _____

Could you please explain briefly how you would help me handle these?

2. Please take a look at the copy of last year's tax return. What tax bracket am I in and what tax rate am I paying on my income sources?

3. What are the latest tax changes that will apply to my and my family's situation this year?

4. What tax provisions should I be carrying forward from previous filing years?

5. How can my family members split income and transfer deductions and credits this year?

6. What are the retirement savings strategies I should be working towards?

7. What new investment strategies should I be considering to take into account tax effectiveness?

8. How can I reduce tax withholding/tax instalment payments this year?

9. How should asset acquisitions and dispositions be timed to make the most tax sense?

10. What audit-proofing procedures should I be putting in place this year?

11. Can you assist me with an audit? How would this be approached?

CHAPTER 3

Building a Productive Advisor/Client Relationship

- **Understand the basics**
- **Communicate quality information to your advisor**
- **Ask the right questions**
- **Coach for results**

How do you become the best coach possible to empower your tax advisor? The key is to have a well-defined game plan, to ask effective questions, to be a good interviewer and to investigate your tax and financial affairs.

To do all of this well, however, you'll need some general tax knowledge, so that you can talk the same language and adjust the game plan to the skill sets of the players and the current environment on the field of play. While you won't be on the field executing the plays, you will be on the sidelines, working together with your team of professional advisors towards a rewarding victory — significant tax savings over your lifetime.

It is likely that one of the reasons you have a tax professional do your taxes in the first place is because you don't want to deal with tax technicalities. However, if one of the reasons you have picked up this book is to take more control of the outcomes of your tax filing procedures, read on to learn more about how to manage and direct your affairs.

You'll need to prepare for your new role by drilling down into some tax filing details, to understand a few rules of the game. This also includes learning some tax lingo. Always remember that tax knowledge is cumulative and best learned when there is a purpose. Because your personal and tax affairs are changing continuously, you can't expect to know it all at once.

Equally important is your ability to communicate to your team the details of your personal tax data for the previous year, including income, family and investment scenarios. You also need to speak about changes in personal circumstances this year as compared to last and how the immediate future will be unfolding. Together with your tax pro's skills and experience, the mix of the two knowledge bases will bring success.

GET THE RESULTS YOU WANT

The first step is to know the field of play. When it comes to your taxes, that's the tax return or the T1 General.

One of the confusing parts about understanding your taxes is that there are so many incarnations of the form itself. There are short forms, internet and TELEFILING questionnaires and a variety of approaches within tax software packages. In fact, one might say that the tax form is now fluid — transcending many incarnations, but culminating in one all-encompassing form: the T1 General. The T1 General, which is always available at the local post office (and is reproduced at the back of this book), can be your anchor ... the reference point or checklist from which you can gather and sort documents.

In order to communicate information about your tax affairs in a mutually understood format to your advisor you'll need to identify the basic elements of the T1 General return.

HOW THE BASIC ELEMENTS OF A TAX RETURN WORK FOR YOU

The T1 General makes reference to all the income, deduction and credit lines you may be entitled to. This is the form your advisor will be using, albeit via a tax preparation package. It has the following six sections of information, plus one set of off-return calculations (item 7 below).

The basic elements of the T1 return are:
1. Your identification
2. Total income
3. Net income
4. Taxable income
5. Federal non-refundable tax credits (Schedule 1)
6. Refund or balance due
7. Refundable tax credits.

These basic elements of the return will be referred to in your correspondence from CCRA (the Notice of Assessment and/or Reassessment, for example) and may be referred to by other tax advisors like your financial planner. They also provide a good skeletal outline and a purpose for defining an introductory interview with your new tax advisor. The following explanations will help you understand the importance of each of these elements so that you can better communicate your wishes surrounding the arrangement of your tax affairs.

Taxpayer Identification

When you first meet with a new tax pro you will want to introduce yourself and your family members, together with certain details your tax pro will need to establish to build each family member's tax filing profile. All tax returns begin with an identification section. Make sure you have Social Insurance Numbers and birthdates handy for all family members filing a tax return for the first time. If you are working with a new advisor, it's also a good idea to bring last year's tax returns for each family member. Your tax pro will ask questions about recent changes to your personal identifiers and your answers will help him map the path of your tax preparation results. Advisor Check-In 3.1 at the end of the chapter outlines what you can expect your advisor to ask about in your initial meeting and Advisor Check-In 3.2 provides a list of questions you may want to ask your advisor to gain an understanding of the importance of the family unit to tax planning.

Tax Query
How is a Spouse or Common-Law Partner Defined?
Before 2001, your spouse for tax purposes was defined as a person of the opposite sex who lived with you in a conjugal (like married) relationship. If you were not legally married, your relationship was conjugal if:
- you lived together throughout a 12-month period ending before December 31 or
- you had a child together (natural or adoptive).

As of January 1, 2001, those who lived common law or who were not of the opposite sex could no longer be referred to as spouse for tax purposes. For them, the term "common-law partner" was coined. So, as a result, provisions that are effective for spouses may also apply to common-law partners who meet the definition above.

Total Income and Your Tax Filing Profile

Your tax advisor will next ask you about your total income. As a Canadian resident, your obligation to report total income for tax purposes includes world-wide income from all sources including barter transactions. Your income will likely fall into one of the following categories:

- employment income
- pension income
- investment income
- other income
- self-employment income.

These income sources can be treated differently for tax purposes. At your introductory interview, you should ask questions about how these sources are taxed so that you can make investment decisions throughout the year that include a view to tax efficiency. This discussion will also help your tax pro understand your tax filing profile, that is whether you are primarily an employee, pensioner, investor, small business owner, student or credit filer and whether you are filing as a single or family unit. To learn about all of your income sources, your advisor will complete an income profile, something like the one in Figure 3.1.

With your income profile in hand, you and your advisor are poised to discuss the changes in your current year's profile, as well as your inter-family tax filing needs. More importantly, you can discuss what tax deductions and credits should be linked to these income sources and how income diversification, income-splitting and income deferral opportunities are available to help you tax cost average over time.

It is a good idea to keep your advisor apprised of any upcoming income variations or potential lump-sum receipts you may be aware of (sale of home, rental property, signing bonus, severance package, inheritance, etc.) since these can have a significant effect on your tax planning.

Attribution Rules

You also need to know that, in general, Canadian taxpayers are not allowed to split income with family members. People sometimes try to do so by transferring assets to spouses and minor children for the purposes of reporting income generated by those assets at those persons' lower tax rates. Unfortunately, this can backfire if you don't know about the attribution rules. You'll find more on that in Chapter 8.

Figure 3.1
Developing an Income Profile

Line	Description	Total
101	Employment Income	
102	Commissions Earned	
104	Other Employment Income	
113	OAS Benefits	
114	CPP Benefits	
115	Other Pensions, Superannuation	
119	Employment Insurance Benefits	
120	Taxable Canadian Dividends	
121	Interest & Other Investment Income	
122	Net Partnership Income	
126	Rental Income	
127	Taxable Capital Gains	
128	Support Payments	
129	RRSP Income	
130	Other Income	
135-143	Self-employment Income	
144-146	Workers' Compensation, Social Assistance, Net Federal Supplements	
150	**Total Income**	

Tax Query
How Much Tax do I Currently Pay on my Total Income Sources?

Ask your advisor to total each of your income sources and then explain how much tax you pay on each. It is also important to understand your marginal tax rate for each. Armed with this knowledge, you may wish to re-balance your investment portfolio to include more tax-efficient income sources or inquire about ways to diversify your income sources or split income with family members to reduce the tax you pay.

Net Income

Net income is a very important figure on your tax return. It is used to compute whether you'll be able to claim certain non-refundable tax credits for supporting your family members and to determine whether you'll get to keep certain social benefits from the government, like Old Age Security, Employment Insurance or receive refundable tax credits like the Canada Child Tax Benefit.

Clawbacks

When we talk about money the government redistributes to its citizens, we usually are confronted with the tax slang: *clawback*. That is, before income is redistributed, the tax system uses a means test, which, in general, is the net income on your individual or your family's tax return. The income number will determine the size of the benefits you'll receive under certain tax provisions. Maximum benefits are reduced or *clawed back* when your income reaches certain levels. Clawbacks could apply to the following benefits; ask your advisor whether any apply to you this year:

- Old Age Security
- Employment Insurance Benefits
- Federal and provincial refundable credits
- Certain non-refundable tax credits including:
  - the age credit
  - the spousal amount
  - amounts for infirm adults 18 and over
  - the caregiver amount
  - medical expenses and charitable donations.

There is another reason, however, that net income is an important figure — one that few people think about, but one which can have significant impact on your family's estate. User fees, like per diem rates paid for personal care or nursing home fees, are based on net income, as are child care space costs in some jurisdictions. A view to reducing net income can help you keep more for your family ... both on and off the tax return.

Taxable Income

This is the figure upon which taxes are calculated for both your federal and provincial governments. The deductions that reduce net income to arrive at taxable income include information about your prior losses, stock option benefits and capital gains deductions.

When your tax advisor talks about your taxable income, know that all definitions of income and deduction are common to both calculations. However, beyond this, your credits for individual family circumstances will differ under federal and provincial tax calculations. It is important to speak to your advisor about the provincial tax implications, especially if you are planning an inter-provincial move any time soon.

Federal Non-Refundable Tax Credits

These can provide you with certain tax breaks for unique family circumstances (e.g., those who support spouses, adult dependants, post-secondary students, charities or the sick and disabled). However, these tax credits only help you if you are paying taxes; they do nothing for those who do not pay.

As a result of your family filing circumstances, you may find that your basic filing profile has many overlaps. Not only do you have to gather information for yourself, but the return also must include information from your spouse and child for some provisions. From an investment point of view, the return may use information from the past or carry information forward to the future.

Therefore, your tax professional will ask for information for individuals within the family and prepare your tax returns as a unit, starting with the lowest earner and working his way up to the highest, in order to maximize transferable tax credit provisions. You'll want to familiarize yourself with tax credits that are claimable by each family member. One way to do so is to ask your advisor to help you complete the chart in Figure 3.2.

Figure 3.2
Which Non-refundable Tax Credits Can My Family Claim?

Credits	Spouse 1	Spouse 2	Dependants
Age			
Spouse			
Equivalent to Spouse*			
Infirm Dependant			
Pension Income			
Caregiver			
Disability			
Tuition/Education			
Medical Expenses			
Donations			
Political Contributions			
LSIF Investments			

*Now called Amount for Qualified Dependant

As these tax credits are constantly changing on both the federal and provincial tax forms and because your personal circumstances could also be changing, it's important that your advisor stay up-to-date with the latest provisions. Ask him to review the highlights of changes for the current year and what changes will affect you in the coming year, at each meeting (see Advisor Check-In 3.3).

In fact, if may be a good idea to schedule quarterly or semi-annual meetings throughout the year to discuss tax changes that apply to your situation as they happen. Keep an eye on the news — federal and provincial budgets, economic statements or newspaper articles that apply to your situation — and initiate a call to your tax advisor if you think there are financial implications for you. Don't be shy about this — it could save you thousands of dollars to consult throughout the year, before you make important personal or financial decisions.

Refund or Balance Due

After all the calculations are completed, this element of the return is of course the one you are most interested in. Use this information to ask some intelligent questions:

- Why was my refund so high? Should I have fewer taxes withheld at source?
- Why did I have to pay so much? Did I not submit enough tax during the year?
- Will I have to make quarterly tax instalment payments during the year?
- Should my tax instalments be reduced as a result of this year's income?

But you should know more. In order to pay the least amount of tax over time, you'll need to understand how much tax you are paying on each income source you earn today. You can then base decisions on the development of tax-efficient income sources and ways to defer tax on income as far into the future as possible.

Now Tax Planning Can Begin

The ability to take control of your future after-tax results begins with an analysis of your tax preparation activities this year ... a crucial concept in financial planning that very few taxpayers understand. The key to making new decisions that drive your after-tax wealth accumulation or preservation begins with an understanding of two terms:

- **Effective Tax Rate.** This is the average rate of tax paid on all income earned this year.
- **Marginal Rate of Tax.** This is the rate of tax paid on the next dollar earned or the tax savings on the next tax deductible dollar spent.

Ask your advisor to identify your marginal tax rate on each source of income or for each tax deductible expenditure you are contemplating. This provides you with useful information that can help you make decisions about how to invest and spend your money. For example, the chart in Figure 3.3 provides tax brackets and the tax rates for different investment income sources.

Figure 3.3

Average Federal and Provincial Marginal Tax Rates on Different Income Sources (2002)

Taxable Income	Income Type		
	Interest	Dividends	Capital Gains
$0–$7,634	0%	0%	0%
$7,635 to $31,677	25%	7%	13%
$31,678 to $63,354	34%	18%	17%
$63,355 to $103,000	41%	26%	21%
Over $103,000	45%	31%	22%

Refundable Tax Credits

The calculations for the last element of the return is largely invisible — the Canada Child Tax Benefit (CCTB) and the Goods and Services Tax/Harmonized Sales Tax Credit (GST/HST Credit). Both of these federal credits are automatically calculated for you by CCRA, but you must file a tax return to receive them. Certain provinces also provide refundable tax credits.

These credits address the costs of raising children, but only for families at certain income levels. Through the use of refundable credits, our tax system does more than just collect tax. It also redistributes taxes collected to provide income supplements to families or reimburse others for GST/HST paid on non-discretionary purchases. For certain families, including those with no self-produced income, filing a tax return is akin to completing an application for government benefits. Such a *negative tax* is targeted to assist low-income individuals and families, but can provide partial benefits to the middle-class.

To make this meaningful to you and your family, find out whether your net family income is within certain income thresholds. You can influence the outcomes of the process by keeping an eye on your RRSP contributions and other deductions leading to net income. These will reduce net income — the figure upon which refundable tax credits are based.

If you do qualify for refundable tax credits, try to have the return filed in such a way that the lower income earner receives them. If the money is subsequently invested by that person throughout the year as the benefits are received, resulting investment earnings are taxed in that person's hands. This is most advantageous if the other earner is in a higher tax bracket.

Maximizing Tax Credits

It is important to understand what your net taxes payable are; that is, how much did you pay after you accounted for the refundable tax credits the government will send back to you. If your family income falls within a claw-back zone, your marginal tax rates can be higher than those borne by higher income earners. It is important to discuss marginal tax rates with your tax advisor in relation to your refundable tax credits.

Your RRSP planning can significantly impact your rights under the refundable tax credit system. For example, if you have a net family income of $45,000 from employment sources, a stay-at-home spouse, no income, two children and live in Ontario, you'll pay federal/provincial taxes of $7,452. You can expect an estimated CCTB of $1,800. If you contribute $5,000 to an RRSP, however, your taxes would go down to $5,894 and your CCTB would go up to about $2,100.

An astute tax advisor would be pointing out that your total savings would be just over $1,800 if you took advantage of your ability to contribute to an RRSP. That's a return on your investment of *36%* — too big a number to ignore, isn't it?

In general, to maximize your non-refundable and refundable tax credits, your tax advisor will be telling you to be sure to claim the following tax deductions which reduce net family income:

- RRSP deductions
- child care expenses
- moving expenses
- investment carrying charges
- employment expenses.

Be sure to provide documentation to support these claims and to arrange your affairs to maximize the appropriate use of these expenditures throughout the year.

THE PAST, PRESENT AND FUTURE

When you take an active interest in your tax preparation affairs, you will take control of your lifetime tax bill, even if someone else prepares your taxes. It is therefore always important to overview your family's returns from an investment point of view and to understand that certain results of your investment decisions, like capital losses, can be carried forward or back to reduce the taxes you are paying on your investment income over a period of years. For that reason, it will be necessary for you to carry information from prior filings into the current tax year. See Advisor Check-In 3.1 for the details.

KNOW THE TAX NEWS

As we mentioned before, it helps to know what's new in tax preparation and to match that with what's new in your life. Ask your advisor to go over the latest tax changes for your situation. See Advisor Check-In 3.3 for a summary of the 2002 tax changes. That's the way to move beyond tax preparation into the zone of tax planning for the future.

TAX PRO COACH
Your Strategic Plan for a Productive Relationship with
Your Tax Advisor

You can't expect your advisor to be able to help you plan for your tax saving future without assistance from you. You must take an active role in building that relationship. Consider the following issues and discuss them with your tax advisor:

- What tax and financial planning decisions should I discuss with my advisor throughout the year?
- What information does my advisor need to help me make those decisions? How do I gather it all together?
- Do I understand the significance of my tax filing profile and those of my family members?
- How can I invest with more tax efficiency?
- How are each of my potential income sources — earned or passive — taxed?
- Do I understand how to keep the most from federal and provincial social benefits available through the tax system?
- How will the investment decisions I made in the past and those I make in the future affect my prior and future tax filing results?
- How are the decisions I make in my family, career, business or investment affairs impacted by taxes?

Advisor Check-In 3.1
Information for Your First and Subsequent Meetings

Your advisor needs to understand many details regarding your lifestyle and your financial decision-making. The items listed below will be vital at your initial meeting and should be reviewed annually.

ABOUT YOU

- Name, address, contact information
- Bring last year's tax returns
- Bring any recent notices from CCRA

QUESTIONS ABOUT YOUR IDENTIFICATION

Your Advisor will Ask	Importance of Your Response
1. Has your marital/living status changed?	You may have become married or divorced and this can affect your refundable and non-refundable tax credits.
2. Has your address changed?	If you have moved at least 40 kilometres you may qualify for moving expenses, or if your province of residence changed, the provincial tax rate will have changed.
3. Do you have a business in another province?	If so, your business will be taxed in that province, requiring a separate tax calculation from your personal affairs.
4. Have you become or ceased to become a Canadian resident?	The personal amounts of immigrants and emigrants must be pro-rated and the fair market value of your assets will have to be assessed for tax purposes.
5. What is your date of birth?	Many provisions on the tax return are dependent upon date of birth, including planning around the reporting of Canada Pension Plan benefits, the RRSP deduction, child care expenses, the Old Age Security benefits repayment, the age credit, amount for infirm dependants age 18 or older, the disability amount, income-splitting provisions with minor children, etc.
6. Is this return for a deceased person?	There are several provisions specific to the final return, including prorated income, and provisions that can be claimed for the year of death and immediately preceding year. You'll also want to know about final RRSP contributions and rules about transfer of assets to family members.
7. What is your marital status?	This is a most important question, as it determines the size of your refundable and non-refundable tax credits and how income can be split with your life partner. It can also determine how children are claimed and by whom.
8. Are you claiming the GST/HST Credit?	It is important to determine who will claim the GST/HST Credit if you are living with a spouse or common-law partner. Generally it is the person with the lower income who should claim this credit.
9. Do you have investments outside of Canada, valued at more than $100,000 (Cdn)? A non-resident trust?	If so, you will have to file a separate form to disclose your foreign holdings and to provide the details of these holdings and dealings to your tax advisor.

ABOUT YOUR INCOME

- Give an account of current year income sources.
- Disclose whether you reported capital gains in the past three years? If so, attach a copy of Schedule 3 for each year in question.
- Disclose whether you reported income from a small business in the past three years. If so, attach a copy of your business statements as well as:
  - Capital cost allowance records: asset acquisition, disposition and depreciation details
  - GST/HST remittances
  - Undeducted business investment losses

ABOUT YOUR ASSETS

Did you acquire assets at any time since 1972? If yes, see below:
- **Real property**
  - supply all documents to prove original cost or value on acquisition
  - supply documents to show all costs of improvements
  - supply documents to show any outlays and expenses, like appraisals
- **Depreciable assets such as buildings, furnishings, equipment or vehicles**
  - supply all documents to prove original cost or value on acquisition
  - value of land must be separated from cost of buildings
  - supply documents to show all costs of improvements
  - supply documents to show any outlays and expenses
- **Shares and mutual funds held outside an RRSP**
  - supply all documents to prove original cost or value on acquisition
  - supply documents to show all reinvestments of distributions
  - supply documents to show any outlays and expenses, like brokerage fees
- **Capital gains elections made in 1994**
  - supply copy of Form T664 (from 1994 tax files)

ABOUT YOUR DEDUCTIONS

Provide information about previous transactions:
- RRSP contributions and unused RRSP room (Schedule 7 and your Notice of Assessment or Reassessment)
- Unused moving expenses (Form T1M)
- Unclaimed capital and non-capital losses of prior years

ABOUT OTHER EXPENDITURES ON SCHEDULE 1

Provide information about the following prior transactions in non-refundable tax credits:
- Unclaimed interest on student loans
- Unclaimed tuition and education credits
- Unclaimed medical expenses of the immediately prior year
- Unclaimed charitable donations from up to five years ago
- Unclaimed Labour-Sponsored Tax Credits from last year
- Unclaimed minimum tax carry-overs

Advisor Check-In 3.2
Introduce Your Family

While Canadians do file tax returns on an individual basis, there are many benefits to taking the family unit into account. Your advisor will know this and will need information about each family member to bring the best tax savings to the family unit as a whole.

A. FAMILY IDENTIFICATION

Name	Birth date	SIN	Phone (Work)	Phone (Cell)	School

- Bring last year's tax return for each family member
- Bring any recent notices from CCRA
- Give an account of current year's income sources

B. Questions to Ask About Your Family Returns

1. When should my minor child file a tax return?
2. When should the following income sources by reported on their returns rather than mine?
   a. Employment income
   b. Interest income
   c. Dividend income
   d. Capital gains income
   e. Wages paid while working for me in my small business
3. What provisions are transferable from my spouse and children to my return?
4. When do the gifts I give my minor children have tax consequences?
5. When should my adult children file tax returns?
6. When can provisions be transferred from my adult child to me?
7. At what income level do I lose my spouse as a dependant?
8. Are there any tax breaks for me if I support other adults in the family?
9. How can I split income with my spouse?
10. How can my spouse and I plan to split retirement income?
11. What provisions can be transferred between spouses?
12. What carrying charges can be claimed as deductions by family members?

Advisor Check-In 3.3
Interpreting Tax News

Ask your advisor how tax changes in 2002 will affect you.

- **Employment Income.** For 2001 and subsequent taxation years, employers may give their employees up to two non-cash gifts per year with a total value not exceeding $500, on a tax-free basis. Ask your tax advisor to help you with a checklist of taxable and tax free perks to ask for the next time you renegotiate your employment contract. Find out whether you qualify for tax-free death benefits or a bonus on your efforts while alive and well.

- **Old Age Security Income (OAS).** The monthly income amounts increased with indexing. As the amount of your OAS income is dependent upon your individual net income, it is important that you understand whether you'll be affected by the clawback of OAS or social benefits repayment. You will be required to pay back some OAS receipts and have OAS benefits reduced in the benefit year starting in July if your individual net income exceeds $56,968 in 2002. Ask your tax advisor to tell you whether you are subject to a clawback and how this will affect the monthly income you will receive from this source in the new benefit year starting in July.

- **Canada Pension Plan Benefits (CPP).** The recipient of the CPP benefits includes them as income. However, if you have a spouse and are 60 or over, you can apply to split the CPP benefits on the tax return. Ask your tax advisor if that makes financial sense in your case. Two "what if" scenarios should be presented to you. Children report orphan's benefits, which increases their net income. This could affect a claim for the amount for eligible dependant (formerly called the equivalent-to-spouse amount).

- **Other Income.** In the year 2000, the exempt amount of scholarship, fellowship or bursary income received was increased from $500 to $3,000 if the student otherwise qualified for the education tax credit. If you missed this, or claimed the wrong amount, ask your tax advisor to claim a tax adjustment for you or the student in your family. This could also have affected how much of the tuition and education credits you qualified to transfer to a higher income earner's return.

- **RRSP Contributions**. There are no changes for the current year; ask your tax advisor about increases in the upper ceiling levels for 2004 ($14,500) and 2005 ($15,500), and how you can maximize your opportunities for tax savings.

- **Child Care Expenses**. If you have a disabled child in the family you may have missed an increase in the child care expense deduction claim. Starting in 2000 expenses up to a maximum of $10,000 per year may be claimed. Adjust your prior-filed returns if you missed this and attach the receipts.

- **Attendant Care Expenses**. This deduction, aimed to reduce net income of disabled individuals who pay an attendant to get ready to work or go to school was expanded in 2000 to be limited to the greater of 2/3 of earned income and the least of that income, $15,000 and $375 times the number of weeks the person was in attendance at a school or educational institution.

- **Moving Expenses**. Many people miss this lucrative tax deduction. After 1997, expenses that were paid in the year after a move may be claimed in the year paid and carried forward for application to a year in which there was income at the new location. If you think that you might be eligible to make these claims in retrospect, ask your tax advisor to adjust your prior filed returns for you.

- **Carrying Charges**. Rules have been relaxed surrounding the documentation and tracing requirements on investment loans. Ask your tax advisor to explain how this affects you if you have made or are considering taking out an investment loan. Also, if you have forgotten to provide your safety deposit box receipts in the past, do so now and ask your advisor to adjust your prior filed returns.

- **Legal Fees Paid for Divorce/Separation**. On October 10, 2002, CCRA published a report in which an important policy surrounding the deductibility of legal fees was changed, and this could be of significant benefit to you if you are contemplating a separation or are having to pay for legal costs to obtain an increase in your support payments. In the past, legal costs incurred to establish the right to spousal support, including the costs of obtaining a divorce, a support order for spousal support under the Divorce Act or a separation agreement were not deductible, as they are considered capital in nature, or are personal or living expenses. In addition, legal costs incurred to obtain an increase in spousal or child support, or to make child support non-taxable were not deductible. As a result of a recent court case (Gallien), CCRA will now consider legal costs incurred to obtain spousal support under the Divorce Act or under provincial legislation in a separation agreement, as well as the costs incurred to obtain an increase in support or make child support non-taxable to be deductible. The new position will not apply retroactively unless a notice of objection was filed and is still outstanding, but will apply for all future assessments after this date. Be sure to ask your tax advisor about this.

- **Net Capital Losses of Other Years.** If you sold stock inside a non-registered account or other assets like land or buildings and incurred an allowable capital loss in the period 1972 to 2001 may be able to use those losses to offset capital gains in 2002. Up to $2,000 of unapplied losses from 1972 to May 22, 1985, may also be applied against other income in 2002. So it is most important for you to look up this information for your tax advisor to save tax dollars this year. Also ask your advisor to identify whether you have incurred losses in 2002 which are going to be applied to capital gains you reported in 1999, 2000, or 2001. If so, ask your advisor to calculate how much you can expect to receive in refunded tax dollars. Then see your financial advisor to invest that windfall wisely.

- **The Basic Personal Amount.** This amount has risen to $7,634 from $7,412. This amount is not transferable to others or from one year to the next so if your income is around $7,600 or less, ask your tax pro how this will affect your RRSP deduction, claims for tuition and education amounts, claims for capital cost allowances if you are a small business owner, or claims for dependants, medical expenses and charitable donations. You'll also need to know about this "tax-free zone" to determine income levels for children who work in your business.

- **The Age Amount**. In 2002 this is $3,728. Know that this amount will be reduced by 15% of your net income over $27,749. The credit will be eliminated totally with income of $52,602. So find out from your tax and financial planning advisors if you can take steps to split income, defer income or diversify your income sources, to stay under those thresholds, and save tax dollars.

- **The Amount for Spouse or Common-Law Partner.** In 2002 this increased to $6,483. The lower net income level is set at $648 with a partial claim allowed for income between $648 and $7,131. By 2004 the spousal amount will not be less than $6,800 with the base income level no less than $680. This is important information for taxpayers who are employing their spouses as assistants in their employment or small business ventures. It is also important from an RRSP planning point of view, as often an RRSP contribution can reduce spousal income below those thresholds to create or increase a spousal amount. Speak to your tax and investment advisors about this. Also remember that starting in 2001, same sex partners are included in the definition for the purposes of this claim.

- **The Amount for an Eligible Dependant**. This amount which supports the costs of single parents in raising their children is equivalent to the spousal amount and operates in a similar fashion. The amount has been increased to $6,483 in 2002. Income between $648 and $7,131 will result in a reduced claim. This amount will not be less than $6,800 by 2004. If you are a recent widow(er) or if you or your spouse has been stricken by disability, find out how CPP orphan's, survivor's or death benefits will affect your income, your claims for your dependants, and your refundable tax credits. Should you be investing in an RRSP to reduce their net income levels? How should you invest this money to ensure that resulting investment earnings are taxed in the recipient's hands? Ask your tax and investment advisors for guidance.

- **Amount for Infirm Dependants over 18.** This has risen to $3,605 in 2002. The dependant's income over $5,115 and under $8,720 will limit the claim. You will want to file a tax return for the disabled adult to generate a GST/HST Credit. You may also want to look at investment strategies for their income sources, if there is enough left over for these purposes. An RRSP (if qualifying earned income is present) or a claim for attendant care deductions (if the disabled person pays this in order to get ready for work or school) can reduce net income.

- **CPP Contribution Rates for Employees**. Employee and employer contribution rates for the year 2002 will increase to 4.7% from 4.3%. Don't be too surprised if you get a refund from over-contributions here … especially if you've had more than one employer and if you turned 18, 70, began receiving CPP retirement benefits or in cases where the taxpayer died. You should plan to add these bonus refunds to your investment capital.

- **CPP Self Employment Rates**. The self-employed contribution rate for 2002 is 9.4% and the maximum self-employed contribution will be $3,346.40. This is often a shock to small business owners, so budget for it.

- **EI Contribution Rates.** Maximum insurable earnings will remain at $39,000, the EI premium rate will drop to 2.2%, and the maximum contribution will be $858. Over-contributions will be refunded via the tax return and once again you should plan to add these to your investment capital, especially if you are always short for RRSP contributions. If you are the owner of a small business, check to see if your family members who work for you will be eligible to collect EI if they ever stop working for you. If not, perhaps you shouldn't be contributing. Talk to your financial advisor about this.

- **Caregiver Amount.** This credit has also increased in 2002 to $3,605. When an individual's net income reaches $15,917 the credit will be eliminated. This credit is meant to assist those who care for adult dependants in their own home. Make sure you ask your tax advisor about this claim … if you missed it in the past, you can file for an adjustment. Also make sure you have been claiming the unreimbursed medical expenses for this dependant.

- **The Disability Amount.** This will rise to $6,180 in 2002. The additional supplement for disabled children will increase to $3,605, however your level of child care expense claims may affect this. Ask your tax advisor to do the calculation a couple of ways to determine your best benefit. The amount is transferable to the higher income supporting individual, and the doctor must sign Form T2201 the first time the claim is made. It may be necessary to file an updated report of the person's condition sometime in the future as well. Ask your tax advisor to adjust prior-filed returns if you find you have missed this beneficial claim. In addition, starting in the year 2000, it was possible to make this claim for those who were otherwise able but receiving life-sustaining out-patient therapy like kidney dialysis or clapping therapy to help with breathing, if therapy was being received at least three times per week and an average of 14 hours per week.

- **Tuition and Education Amount.** Beginning in 2002, students who receive financial assistance for post-secondary education under government training programs such as the Employment Insurance Act or any other training program established under the authority of the Human Resources Development Commission will qualify for the tuition and education amount. Otherwise be sure to ask your tax advisor to review your prior-filed returns to ensure that you have claimed your tuition and education amounts properly. Especially if your income has hovered between $6,500 and $7,500, it is possible that your tuition and education credits were transferable to a spouse, parent or grandparent, or that you can carry the unused amounts forward for use in your future filings. If you lived and filed in Manitoba, remind your tax advisor of the learning tax credit that was available up until 2001. Be sure to file for this as well.
- **Tuition and Education Amount Transferred from a Child.** No change for 2002; however, do know that many people miss this transfer. If you suspect you did, discuss your prior filing results with your tax advisor.
- **Medical Expenses.** Maximum reduction in medical expenses (3%) rises from $1,678 to $1,728. Medical expenses are often missed or filed incorrectly. It should be the spouse with the lower net income who makes the claim, if that person is taxable, for a better result. You should also ask your tax advisor to claim medical expenses incurred in the best 12-month period ending in the tax year … which means you'll have to bring along unclaimed medical bills over the past two years to help your pro maximize your claim. Be sure to bring proof of all reimbursements from public/private health care as well. Also know that starting in 1999, it was possible to use a simplified method of claiming auto expenses for those who have to travel for medical treatments. Speak to your tax advisor about this.
- **Schedule 1: Minimum Tax Carry-over.** If you had unusually high income in the past, it is critical to check back over the past seven years (2001 back to 1996) to see if you may have paid a minimum tax amount. If so, you can possibly use this amount to reduce your taxes payable this year. Many taxpayers and their advisors forget to check for this, so prompt your tax advisor by asking about it this year. Then keep the carry forward information current in a permanent tax file.
- **Federal Tax Rates and Brackets for 2002.** It is important for you to ask your tax advisor whether your income is hovering around any of these bracket thresholds. You need to understand at what level your next dollar of income earned will be taxed, in order to make wise financial planning decisions:

Taxable Income	Federal Tax Rates
$0–$7,634	0%
$7,635 to $31,677	16%
$31,678 to $63,354	22%
$63,355 to $103,000	26%
Over $103,000	29%

CHAPTER 4

Tax Filing Time: Goodbye Shoebox

- Prepare a quick sort of receipts
- Know what permanent information must be kept
- Conduct a tax prep interview to meet your info needs
- Keep information retrievable for audit

Did you know that the majority of North Americans spend an average of ten to 13 hours preparing their annual tax returns? Considering that the actual data entry and tax calculations often take only several minutes — especially if you are using tax software — that's a big slice out of your busy life.

Worse still, it appears that the majority of the time is spent on the frustrating stuff — looking for tax receipts, forms and information to prepare the return, instead of quality time working with your tax advisor to find tax deductions and credits and plot long-term tax savings. Dealing with this documentation burden is the first step to saving time and money.

Most people have a hard time with the assembly of their tax records because they do not have a specific place to keep receipts and slips as they arrive during the year. So slips are left near the phone, others are taken up to the home office, more languish on the night table next to the bed and still more are stuck in the glove compartment in the car. Come tax time, there is a mad scramble to retrieve receipts from five or six probable receipt-hoarding locations — none of which are actually there when you really need them.

But the tax deadline does drive us into collective action: found receipts are hastily fired into a shoebox, candy jar or fishbowl for the tax preparer.

Small business people or commission sales people often graduate to the dreaded accordion file. (You can be sure, when your professional tax preparer sees the accordion file, she is swallowing hard before looking inside and starting the fees meter!)

Here's the good news ... you don't have to be an expert at tax law or policy to present information that empowers your tax advisor at tax time. All you have to do is three things:

1. Communicate and support all the relevant information about your individual/family life, career or business and investment transactions of the past year.
2. Ask questions that will allow you to maximize your deductions and credits and set up tax savings measures for the future.
3. Retrieve information from the past that may apply to reduce your taxes this year. This is especially important during a tax audit or if you have changed tax advisors.

But to do so, you have to make a commitment. Your tax receipts will be held in one place only and you will get into the habit of using that designated receipt receptacle faithfully throughout the year.

Most taxpayers resist the initial effort required to set up a filing system, but if you are working with a tax advisor it is well worthwhile. Once you have your system set up it requires limited effort to maintain it. And doing so puts you in a much stronger position to ensure you are maximizing the benefit of paying an advisor.

For example, as you go about your business, you may find that you have tax-oriented questions to ask your tax pro about your career directions or the financial implications of family health management. Or you may wish to speak to your financial advisors about changes in your investment portfolio. By having access to properly filed documents, you'll be able to easily retrieve them for reference throughout the year, as well as during your annual tax prep interview. This will allow you to take advantage of the year-round services your tax preparation fee usually includes and, more importantly, to make better decisions that can lead to tax savings.

If you are ready to make the commitment to take control of the taxes you pay, the simple sorting procedures that follow will be as empowering for you as they will be for your professional advisors.

THE TAX RECEIPT RECEPTACLE

Tax receipts come to you daily — when you buy gas, pay for lunch, park, pick up the mail, buy gifts for your clients. Take the receipts out of your

wallet or daybook and put them straight into your tax receptacle daily or weekly. This receptacle must have the following characteristics:
- It must be able to hold a half a dozen file folders per tax filer.
- It must have a lid or other closed top.
- It should be easily transportable.
- You must be able to neatly label it and stack it away with this year's tax return after it has been prepared.

Begin your separation from the shoebox by buying a filing cabinet or a cardboard filing box. Then put it in a place where you will use it every day or at least once a week.

WHAT TO KEEP

In your annual tax interview, your tax preparation professional needs to get an overview of your filing situation quickly and completely. She'll need to understand what income sources and offsetting deductions you have this year, how your individual return interacts with your family's and how your investment transactions influence your tax results from yesterday, today and tomorrow. Your tax pro also needs to understand what is different in your life — career and family — and match that to what's changed in tax law and policy. By taking responsibility for an orderly presentation of information you can really help your tax pro help you.

Be sure to ask your tax professional about how she would like you to keep information and to give you a general overview of important documentation specific to your current situation and transactions you are contemplating in the future.

THE PROCESS — A PRIMARY SORT

The general rule is this: when in doubt, keep it all, but keep it in order! It is most important that you have all of your documents for income and expenditures, as well as investment transactions. However, it is also most helpful to keep documents within a primary sort, so that your tax accountant can work from a recognizable skeletal order and flesh out the body of your return logically, according to the tax forms Canada Customs and Revenue Agency (CCRA) mandates and with a minimal effort.

There are only three steps and six folders required to saving time and money on gathering up your tax receipts under the primary sort.

1. **Year Long.** To sort receipts, create four topical folders. For a quick sort, drop receipts into these folders on a daily or weekly basis.

2. Once a Year. Update your permanent file which carries information your tax advisor needs to access from year-to-year.

3. At Tax Time. Prepare your family file to help your advisor understand the economic decision-making within the family unit.

This simple system will not only keep your advisors from groaning when they see you rush in on April 29, but the discipline to live within a three-step solution to your bookkeeping woes will help you make tax-wise decisions on career, family and investment opportunities all year long.

Year Long — the Quick Sort

You will likely have noticed that the records you received during the year fall into four broad categories:

1. investments
2. business records
3. other income
4. other expenditures.

Open four file folders each labelled as above. Then fire your receipts and documents into these four folders, as appropriate, throughout the year. If the records become too plentiful, open secondary folders as appropriate.

Your Investments

In your investment folder, file anything you receive from your financial institutions, broker, financial advisors — any place you have opened an account and invested money. This also will include your RRSP, RRIF, RESP or other registered savings and your non-registered investments. Also include any information about the expenses you incur to make your investments, including:

- interest on bank loans or loans from your employer or business
- safety deposit box fees
- investment counsel fees
- inter-family loans.

You may also have records of transactions surrounding other investments, such as the sale of land or houses, rental properties, farms, artwork, etc. or receipts from the improvements to your cottage. Be sure to put the documents for any transactions surrounding these items into this folder. Finally, put your personal bank statements and credit card statements into this folder.

Your Business Records

There are four types of documents you'll fire into this folder:
- income received or receivable
- expenses paid or payable, including auto log
- assets acquired or disposed of
- bank statements and credit card statements.

If there are lots of documents, you may wish to break these records down into four secondary folders labelled business income, business expenses, business assets and business banking/credit cards. Put the receipts you collect into the appropriate folder. Proprietors or commission sales people would prepare business file records similar to what is described here.

Your Other Income

Generally, other income sources are reported to you throughout the year via a stub of some kind: a cheque stub, a stub from a cashed-in RRSP, a receipt for a bursary, a payroll record stub, a withdrawal slip, etc. Drop these into your other income folder as they come in.

Your Other Expenditures

No matter what you spend money on, put your receipts into this folder. This can include charitable donations, medical expenses, child care, political contributions, tuition fees, etc. Any other expenses that are not investment- or business-related are deposited into this file.

To help you assemble these four folders, see Figure 4.1, Everything In Its Place. You can use the checklists of information under each primary topic as a guideline to saving receipts or as a cover file behind which receipts are filed.

Once A Year — the Permanent File

Important information must be carried forward on an annual basis for use by your tax professional. This will include two groups of transactions:

1. **Current Tax Year and Three Years Back.**
- Record of instalment tax, source or GST/HST remittances made during the year.
- Copies of Notices of Assessment or Reassessment from this year and the prior three years.
- Copy of your prior-filed tax returns (three years back).

Figure 4.1:
Everything in Its Place

This system will keep your year-long quick sort organized and fast. Set up the file folders according to the headings here and then simply find and file all year.

A. INVESTMENT FOLDER

- RRSP contribution or withdrawal receipts
- Labour-Sponsored Fund Investments or redemptions: federal and provincial
- T Slips: T3, T5, T4PS, etc. Attach your copies in order.
- Other investment account transactions, statements from financial institutions
- Other assets: receipts regarding acquisition, disposition or improvement of capital assets
- Records of losses on private or public shareholdings (i.e., evidence that your investment is worthless)
- Records of stock options granted and exercised
- Carrying charges: interest expenses, brokerage fees, spousal loans, safety deposit boxes, etc.
- Self-reported investment sources: partnerships, mortgages, notes held, guarantees, etc.
- Rental properties: income and expense records (one folder per property)
- Bank and credit card statements

B. BUSINESS FOLDER

- All income deposit, barter or cash receipts records
- Asset acquisition and disposition receipts
- Business journals, time and appointment journals
- Expense records, receipts and notes of expenditures, including:
    - Auto expenses and distance log
    - Business license, professional memberships, insurance
    - Communications: Internet and telephone
    - Meals and entertainment
    - Office rent or home office expenses including utilities and repairs
    - Office supplies
    - Promotional expenses, travel costs
    - Training and professional development
    - Salary, wages, sub-contracting including amounts paid to family members
    - Sales taxes collected and remitted (record of payment and acceptance)
    - Source deductions collected and remitted (record of payment and acceptance)

C. OTHER INCOME FOLDER

- T Slips from employment income
- T Slips for Canadian public pension (Old Age Security and Canada Pension Plan)
- T Slips for private pensions (superannuation, annuities, RRSP or RRIF)
- T Slips for Employment Insurance (EI), federal supplements, Workers' Compensation
- Other income from: partnerships, scholarships, tips, casual earnings, foreign income, etc.
- Taxable support payments received
- Documentation for foreign pension income received and exchange rates
- Exempt income like:
  - refundable tax credits receipts and reinvestment information
  - death benefits of employment
  - court settlements for damages
  - foster parents payments
  - gifts or inheritances
  - sweepstakes, gambling, other winnings in games of chance
  - life insurance policy proceeds
  - RRSP withdrawals under the Lifelong Learning Plan or Home Buyers' Plan

D. OTHER EXPENDITURES FOLDER

- Receipts for union dues or professional dues
- Child care costs including nursery and day camps, attendant care costs
- Moving expenses
- Employment expenses: auto, home office, travel, sales and promotion
- Repayments of EI or other benefits
- Tuition, education costs including student loan interest
- Medical expenses for the last two years
- Charitable donations and political contributions: federal and provincial
- Record of instalment tax, source remittances or GST/HST remittances made during the year

2. **Farther Back.**
- Any supporting documents carried forward from prior years' business statements: asset records, home office carry-overs, details of share ownership, etc.
- Supporting documents to assets and investments: RRSP contribution history, cost base information, value of gifts, inheritances, other asset transfers to you, dispositions of prior years that resulted in losses carried forward.
- Unused past personal provisions: charitable donations, moving expenses, home office or other provisions still unused from the past.

- Capital gains elections made in 1994 — copy of Form T664 from your 1994 tax files.
- Record of private health insurance premiums paid this year and back as far as 1968.

This information is best gathered using Advisor Check-In 4.1. Ask your tax pro to help you update this file every year.

At Tax Time — Family Filing

When you see your tax advisor at tax time you will be asked for certain information about your family members. This is so that the tax preparer can begin with the return of the lowest income earner and work her way up to the highest earner. This information also allows the preparer to do your family unit's returns to your best benefit, using all transferable tax provisions possible. It will also help you work more effectively with your financial advisors in making decisions about family investments. Use Advisor Check-In 4.2 to help you with the task of gathering the appropriate family information.

SET UP AN ANNUAL TAX PREP INTERVIEW

A key reason to invest time in meticulous document storage and retrieval is to empower you and your advisor to ask some intelligent questions of one another, so that you can make and save money on your taxes in the future. The onus is on you to lead the process by presenting the information in a manageable way. Now communications with your advisor can begin in a useful, two-way process.

Effective data harvesting, therefore, leads directly to the tax preparation interview. This is a critical part of successful tax preparation in the current year and tax savings initiatives for the future. If you are not taking the opportunity to have such an interview, ask for it. If it is not available, you likely should be looking for someone else to help you with your tax preparation.

Your tax preparer should have been trained to interview you in a skilful manner to extract all the relevant tax information required to prepare your taxes quickly, completely and to your best benefit. If you are wise and goal-oriented, you will be cross-examining. Using the properly presented documentation as a guide, your goal should be to extract information equally as skill- fully from your tax advisor to help you make tax and money-saving decisions.

Preparing Your Questions

As you gather up your documents, be sure to keep a note pad near by to jot down the questions you wish to ask of your tax and financial advisors. First, get a handle on your income and how it is taxed. Then ask some intelligent questions about tax savings opportunities in the future. See Advisor Check-In 4.3 for some guidance on the sort of questions you should be asking.

Figure 4.2
Audit-Readiness Test

Line on Return	Documentation Required
126 Rental Income	Income earned, expenses of operation, capital acquisitions and improvements or repairs
127 Capital Gains	Proceeds of disposition, adjusted cost base, and the source of outlays and expenses are often audited.
128 Support Payments	Your agreement and records of payment received.
135 Self Employment	Bank records to support income, hard copy for expenses and capital acquisitions.
208 RRSP Deduction	All receipts, sorted in date of purchase order and a record of carry-over provisions.
214 Child Care Expenses	Receipts for all payments made.
215 Attendant Care Expenses	Receipts for payment to an attendant.
217 Business Investment Loss	Statements describing the details of the loss, when it occurred and how any unapplied balances have been used to offset income in prior years.
219 Moving Expenses	Form T1M and all receipts for amounts claimed on this form.
220 Deductible Support	Records for amounts actually paid for the support under the agreement's terms.
221 Carrying Charges	Receipts for all amounts claimed here including safety deposit boxes, and the details of loans taken for investment purposes. Any dual-purpose loans must be prorated (i.e. personal and investment use).
229 Employment Expenses	Receipts for all expenses claimed, plus form T2200 Declaration of Conditions of Employment.
316/318/326 Disability Amount	Form T2201 Disability Amount Certificate signed by the doctor.
323/324 Tuition and Education Amounts	Form T2202A is required, issued by the institution.
330 Medical Expenses	Receipts to verify claims for all unreimbursed expenses.
349 Donations	Receipts must bear official registration numbers from charitable organizations and should be grouped to exceed the $200 threshold for a higher claim.

KEEPING THE INFO AUDIT-READY

Finally, remember that you are collecting and storing data for yet another reason: to comply with CCRA requirements and be in a position to answer questions about how you filed your return if you are selected for audit. So once your advisor has completed your tax preparation for another year, put your return through the quick audit test (see Figure 4.2, Audit-Readiness Test).

Refer to the list of frequently audited lines on the tax return from Figure 4.2 and pick three of these lines used on your tax return. Try to find the supporting documentation for these three lines. If you can easily retrieve the information and match the numbers on the return with the actual receipts in your files, you have passed the audit test and should now carefully store the information for future retrieval. Be sure it is labelled with the current tax year easily visible.

Remember having a tax pro doesn't absolve you of responsibility. So do this quick check for your own peace of mind.

TAX PRO COACH
Your Strategic Plan for Document Management to Empower Your Tax Pro

Now that the reasons are clear for setting up a document sorting system, plan a meeting to discuss this information retrieval system with your tax professional. Consider the following issues before you meet with your advisor.

- Is my document sorting system in sync with my advisor's understanding of my tax filing and tax planning needs?
- How can I work with my advisor to understand my tax filing options and ensure I'm saving all the right documents?
- Do I understand how I should store and retrieve the information for tax audit purposes?

Advisor Check-In 4.1
Your Individual Permanent Tax File

A. YOUR INDIVIDUAL IDENTIFYING INFORMATION

Name	Birthdate	SIN	Phone (Work)	Phone (Cell)	Marital Status

B. CARRY-FORWARD INFORMATION

Include in this file:

Group 1:   Current Tax Year and Three Years Back:

- Copies of Notices of Assessment or Reassessment from this year and the prior three years
- Copy of your prior-filed tax returns (three years back)

Group 2:   Farther Back:

- Any supporting documents carried forward from prior years' business statements: asset records, home office carry-overs, details of share ownership, etc.
- Supporting documents to assets and investments: RRSP contribution history, cost base information, value of gifts, inheritances, other asset transfers to you; dispositions of prior years that resulted in losses carried forward.
- Unused past personal provisions: charitable donations, moving expenses, home office or other provisions still unused from the past.
- Capital gains elections made in 1994 — Copy of Form T664 from 1994 tax files.

C. OTHER DOCUMENTATION

You will need to provide other information and documentation also, so dig through that shoebox to locate these pieces of data:

- Your RRSP carry forward information
- Details of your employment contract (attach pay stubs, employment contract)
- Details of separation agreement (attach separation agreement, divorce settlement)
- Your Registered Pension Plan (RPP)
- Your capital losses (record capital losses in prior years from asset dispositions)
- Non-capital loss carry-overs (did you have any non-capital or business loss balances?)
- Business investment loss carry-overs (attach statement from year of original loss)
- Limited partnership loss carry-overs (attach statement from year of original loss)
- Asset acquisition record (did you buy or receive any assets in the past year?)
- Mortgages, commercial, or loans held with family members, and guarantees held

Advisor Check-In 4.2
Family and Investment Information: Current Year

In order to complete your tax return to the best benefit of your family unit, your tax pro will need some information about your family as well as all your details. Keep this information up-to-date.

A. FAMILY — PERMANENT FILE

Name	Birthdate	SIN	Student	Details of Infirmity	Details of Employment	Work/Cell Phone

Keep this information in each family member's permanent file.
Bring the permanent file along with each member's topical file folders to your meeting with your tax professional.

B. FAMILY DATA
Bring each family member's topical file folders and permanent file.

C. INTER-FAMILY INVESTMENT SUMMARY
Describe the total principal invested during the year. Ask your financial advisor, broker or investment house to provide information about your non-registered investments and attach purchase, sale and transfer documents for other capital transactions. You'll need to provide information on:
- RRSPs
- RPPs
- RESPs
- Interest-bearing capital
- Dividend-producing capital
- Other equities
- Unrealized capital gains or losses

Advisor Check-In 4.3
Sample Questions for Annual Tax Prep Meeting

When preparing for your annual tax preparation meeting with your tax pro, remember to jot down questions you want to ask as you gather up your documents. Here are some samples to get you started.

QUESTIONS ABOUT MY CONJUGAL RELATIONSHIPS AND FAMILY

1. What effects does a common-law relationship have on my taxes?
2. When is the best time to get married, from a tax point of view?
3. What tax provisions exist to acknowledge the expense of raising a family?
4. How do I properly keep child care expense receipts? What should be kept? What's not allowed?
5. What receipting is required to make a claim for tuition fees and costs of education?
6. Is there a right time, tax wise, to finalize a separation or divorce? What documentation is required?
7. Is the monthly payment I get from my ex-spouse for myself and my children taxable? What documentation is required?
8. May I contribute to my RRSP based on the payments I receive for support and maintenance of myself and my child? When can I do this and what documents does my financial advisor require?
9. Can I claim my spouse or children as dependants in the year of separation/divorce?
10. What happens if I separate from my spouse and then get back together?
11. What medical expense receipts should be kept?
12. Which charitable donations slips are claimable; which are not?

EMPLOYMENT-RELATED QUESTIONS

1. What is my RRSP contribution room and how much have I over- or under-contributed?
2. What is the optimal amount I should contribute to my RRSP for last year?
3. What forms need to be filed in order for me to claim my out-of-pocket expenses of employment?
4. What out-of-pocket expenditures are deductible?
5. What documentation is required for me to properly show payments made to my spouse for my employment purposes?
6. How can I reduce the tax withholding charges my employer makes every two weeks?
7. What medical receipts do I have to keep and how do I show the portion not covered by my employer's group health plan?
8. What documents are required to make a claim for home office or auto expenses?

INVESTMENT-RELATED QUESTIONS

1. What documents are required to show RRSP contributions from the past that have not yet been deducted?
2. What documents are required to report capital or non-capital losses of the past?
3. How do I show that an investment I have made in shares of a private small business corporation are worthless now and when do I write off the loss?

4. How to I report losses in a limited partnership investment?
5. How do I report the interest that I pay for investment loans, if that interest expense is part of a larger line of credit that I have with the bank?
6. How do I link my interest expenses and other carrying charges to my investments?
7. What information do you need to file an adjustment for the safety deposit box charges I have missed claiming for the past several years?
8. What documents do you require for me to prove the fair market value of assets I have acquired or disposed of?
9. How can I split my investment income with other family members to take advantage of their tax-free zones and lower tax rates?
10. Can I reduce my tax bill by making different investments?

BUSINESS-RELATED QUESTIONS

1. What documentation is needed to show payments to family members who work in the business?
2. What is the difference between a subcontractor and employee; what documentation is required?
3. What documentation must be presented to verify all income is reported?
4. How should auto expense logs be kept?
5. How should business networking journals and expense justification be documented?
6. How do I justify the fair market valuations of my asset transfers?
7. How are income tax, GST/HST and excise tax audits connected and how do I ensure all records for each type of potential audit check out?

CHAPTER 5

Life Events and their Tax Impact

■ **Know what life events can impact on your taxes**
■ **Record changes in your family situation**
■ **Plan for significant milestones for you and your family**
■ **Plan long-term wealth accumulation or preservation strategies with your advisor**

Birth, marriage, death, separation or divorce, university entrance, sale of business, unemployment, illness, career change, self-employment, inheritances, even certain birthdays — all of these life events can have tax consequences. Yet many taxpayers miss significant tax saving opportunities because they don't keep their advisors informed about personal change.

Whenever possible, taxpayers and their advisors should get together *before* personal milestones occur to discuss their tax consequences. Become familiar with the events that can influence your taxes. Embrace a process of tax effective, life-goal planning before retirement, disability or death. You could save hundreds, if not thousands, of dollars if you think tax first, as you and your family approach significant milestones in your lives. For this reason, it is important to work with a professional who is there for you all year long.

One way to ensure you ask all the right tax questions of your tax advisor and then take the right perspective in planning your financial affairs is to "think tax" at every birthday in the family. There are six age milestones to watch for:

- birth to age 6
- ages 7 to 16
- ages 17 and 18
- ages 19 to 29
- ages 30 to 59
- ages 60 plus

Figure 5.1 outlines the tax significance of each of these milestones. Family investment profiles are discussed in more detail in Chapter 8.

Figure 5.1
Age Milestones with Tax Significance

Milestone	Tax Significance
Birth to Age 6	• Enhanced Canada Child Tax Benefits (CCTB) available
	• Enhanced child care expense claims possible
	• Enhanced disability tax credit possible
	• Planning: open CCTB accounts; separate accounts for gifts from non-resident grandparents — both are free from the attribution rules
	• Gift capital-gains producing assets to otherwise avoid attribution
	• Open Registered Education Savings Plan (RESP) accounts to earn up to $400 Canada Education Savings Grant (CESG) Credits
Age 7–16	• Child care expense claim reduced but still possible
	• CCTB reduced but still possible
	• Create Registered Retirement Savings Plan (RRSP) room by reporting all employment/self-employment
	• Continue to invest in RESP
	• Continue to deposit CCTB into untainted savings account
Ages 17 and 18	• File return to position taxpayer to receive GST/HST Credit right after 19th birthday
	• Canada Pension Plan (CPP) premiums become payable the month after the 18th birthday
	• CCTB ends
	• CESG eligibility ends
	• Eligibility for spousal equivalent amount ends
Ages 19 to 29	• GST/HST Credit becomes payable the quarter after the individual turns 19
	• Post-secondary school bound: report scholarships, RESP income, tuition/education amounts, student loan interest
	• Conjugal relationships begin: income-splitting, RRSP spousal investments, principal residence rules
	• Home Buyers' Plan and Lifelong Learning Plan under RRSP may be activated

Age 30 to 59	• Peak productivity: RRSP maximizations; tax-efficiency in non-registered savings, business start rules important
	• Tax-wise employment negotiations important
	• Family problems: consequences on divorce, illness and death
	• Charitable and legacy planning: annual updates required
	• Parental care: caregiver amounts, medical expenses
Age 60 plus	• Retirement income sources change tax paying profile
	• Pension withdrawal planning; clawback zones
	• Sale of taxable and non-taxable assets
	• Transfer of property with the family
	• Split CPP income with spouse
	• Old Age Security (OAS) begins at age 65; new age credit; spousal transfers
	• 69: plan to make taxable withdrawals from RRSP at age 70; make spousal RRSP contribution if you have unused room and spouse is under age 69
	• Check instalment payment requirements annually

PLANNING FOR KEY LIFETIME EVENTS

It is important that you manage the key decisions of your lifetime and the milestones surrounding your nuclear family with the assistance of your financial advisors. Many tax professionals don't charge for this extra help throughout the year. That year-round consultation service is often included in your tax preparation or financial consultant's fee. Be sure to take advantage of this. Refer to Advisor Check-In 5.1 at the end of this chapter for questions to review with your advisor around each personal milestone coming up in the near future for yourself and your nuclear family.

This sort of preparation will help you make better decisions, have more confidence and experience less fear as you encounter significant life events. In short, you'll be in control of your destiny with well-researched, discussed and documented plans. When it comes to your taxes, you'll also save more money, which translates into enhanced wealth creation over time.

It is interesting to note that sometimes the most stressful of life events trigger large lump sums of new capital, like life insurance proceeds, severance or equity from the disposition of property. To make difficult decisions around what must be sold, transferred, invested or managed when the mind is full with other things — death, divorce, moves, critical illness — is a tremendous challenge. This is when you really need a competent team of tax and financial advisors in your court.

The key lifetime events to trigger tax consequences include the following:
• illness and disability
• separation or divorce
• death
• early retirement or termination
• emigration
• gifting during one's lifetime
• transfers of assets and gift-giving after death
• marital status
• starting a new job
• entrepreneurship.

When you encounter one of these events meet with your advisor to discuss how best to proceed, but there are some general concepts you should be familiar with first, as described in the following sections. Then consult Advisor Check-In 5.2 for important questions to ask of your advisors surrounding each of these events.

When Illness or Disability Strike

At a time when long-term illness or disability strikes, lump sums can be received retroactively from wage loss replacement plans, Canada Pension Plan disability benefits or from the sale of residences and vacation properties, vehicles or personal properties. Many questions may arise: How much of this new money can be retained for other purposes? How much must be added to taxable income? When is the best time to receive it, from a tax point of view, if you have a choice? How is it to be managed to be maximized?

Several tax credits and other preferences may now be available, such as the disability amount or the caregiver amount. New expenditures may also abound, including the costs of providing care for the patient, medical treatments, devices or drugs or costs incurred to rebuild or renovate the family home to better adapt it for a person with a disability. When things are better, expenses relating to the opening of a home-based business or for attendant care to help the person who is disabled return to work or school may be available for income reducing purposes.

Your advisor will know how these costs can be recovered — or partially recovered — with help from the tax system. Ask your advisor to prepare several "what if" scenarios that will help you to make the right decisions for your time and money. To get you started with your advisor, refer to Advisor Check-In 5.2 for some questions regarding illness and disability.

Before Separation or Divorce

When a couple gets separated or divorced, new money is received from liquidation of family residences, splitting of registered and non-registered investments or changing children's education funds. The details of support payments for spouse and children must be negotiated and their tax consequences determined. A new look is required at tax brackets and effective and marginal tax rates so that investment strategies can be reviewed. It is most important at this time to speak to tax, legal, insurance and investment planners and preferably for these professionals to be in sync with each other's advice for this situation. Your tax advisor should provide you with several "what if" scenarios to help you assess the tax costs or benefits of each option available in your settlement. The ideal scenario is to ensure that the lives of dependants continue relatively uninterrupted after the change and at the same — or better — after-tax cost. Advisor Check-In 5.2 will provide you with some questions regarding separation and divorce to cover with your advisor.

Tax Implications of Death

When there is a death in the family, there are immediate tax consequences. First, all assets are considered disposed of immediately before the time of death. Those assets can be rolled over to a surviving spouse, often with no tax consequences. Or one can choose to generate some specific tax consequences to take advantage of certain provisions in the final year, like writing off losses or maximizing the use of non-refundable tax credits on several elective returns. The directives in the will generate most of the tax consequences relating to ownership of assets and determine who gets income and investment streams and non-taxable gifts. However, it is possible that certain designations can be made for RRSP and RRIF roll-overs, for example.

There are also several implications for the tax returns of survivors. New sources of capital can be received from tax-exempt life insurance policy benefits. These should be invested, but get advice on the tax-efficiency of resulting investment income. Death benefits from the deceased's employer may be received (up to $10,000 is considered tax free in certain cases). In addition, there is the tax-free roll-over of certain assets and registered pension plan deposits to a spouse, receipt of the lump-sum CPP death benefit, CPP survivor's or orphan's benefits, the taxable transfer of other property to trusts, children, grandchildren — all will require thought and professional guidance as family tax filing profiles will change. Your tax advisor will want to prepare "what if" scenarios to find out the most advantageous way to set up dispositions and new adjusted cost bases of inherited assets so that tax is minimized both now and in the future. This topic is discussed in more detail in Chapter 10 and Advisor Check-In 5.2 provides some questions to explore with your advisor.

Managing Early Retirement or Severance

Severance packages, access to public and private pension plans, employment insurance, the need for medical and other group insurance benefits, depletion of non-registered accounts, new tax instalment payments, the start of a consulting practice — all of these circumstances can stem from an early retirement or job termination. It is important to structure income under the new reality carefully. For example, your goal is to preserve as much of the severance package as possible, by taking advantage of the possibility of rolling over a certain amount to RRSPs or maximizing unused RRSP contribution room available, and to ensure you keep all of your Employment Insurance benefits. You will also need to understand how your new tax filing profile will co-mingle with that of other family members as you may now qualify for tax credits that were prohibited due to the size of your income in the past. Advisor Check-In 5.2 provides some more questions and issues to explore with your advisor.

Before Leaving the Country

The Canadian government requires the reporting of all taxable assets before you leave and payment of resulting taxes. Liquidation of Canadian holdings in order to emigrate or become a permanent non-resident may have tax consequences. However, when there is no actual disposition, a *deemed disposition* is considered to have taken place for tax purposes, based on the fair market value of those assets at the date of departure. As many who departed just before the bear market can attest, choosing the departure date will have big bearings on your disposition values and your after-tax results.

Exempt from the requirement to report a deemed disposition upon emigration are: real property situated in Canada, capital property used in a business situated in Canada, excluded rights such as accumulations in RRSPs, RRIFs, RESPs, employee profit sharing plans, superannuation and other private and public pension plans, retiring allowances and rights under stock options. None of these situations will be subject to the departure taxes.

Also, there are no tax reporting requirements on the disposition of the principal residence or on personal use property with a value under $10,000. Emigrants who hold property with a value of more than $25,000 must complete a prescribed form by April 30 after departure: Form T1161 List of Properties by an Emigrant.

Emigrants may choose to post security in lieu of paying the departure taxes on these deemed dispositions, so that they can pay the taxes when they actually sell the property. Interest on the outstanding taxes will not be charged on amounts equal to taxes payable on the first $100,000 of capital gains, security is not required.

Taxpayers who return to Canada may request that departure taxes be refunded to them. Also, if after emigration, the property declines in value, emigrants will have paid taxes on paper gains that did not materialize. In that case, a special loss carry-back will be allowed at the time of actual disposition to recover overpaid taxes at departure.

So, it is critical to speak about the tax consequences of emigration well before the date is chosen and to have your tax advisor perform several "what if" scenarios to help you finalize your departure tax strategies and your departure date.

Give with Tax Advantages

Gifts

Cash or property gifted during one's lifetime by those who are liquidating assets may have a variety of tax consequences depending on what is given and to whom. There are two things to consider:

- Will there be a capital gain or loss on the deemed disposition that occurs upon transfer of the property?
- To whom will income resulting from the transferred asset be taxed after the transfer?

Your tax advisor will be able to explain the rules and the impact of each situation.

Transfer of Assets, Gift-Giving after Death

When a taxpayer dies, it is very important for surviving family members to receive tax and investment advice immediately. However, because of the stress of the event, it is most important to ensure that no major financial decisions are undertaken in the first year after the death of a loved one without professional advice of at least a couple of individuals: tax accountants, lawyers and financial planners. In fact, it is best for all concerned when the financial planning occurs before death. That process should involve pre- and post-death "what if" scenarios developed by the tax pro. For more information, and tax questions to discuss with your advisor, see Advisor Check-In 5.2 and Chapter 10.

Marriage Requires a New Tax Focus

What basic income, deduction and credit information needs to be discussed with your advisor to make sure you maximize your claims for special circumstances within the family? These discussions should begin when a new conjugal relationship is entered into. This can include legal marriage or the common-law unions of members of the same or opposite sex. This topic is discussed in detail in Chapter 3.

Before Landing a New Job
Salary, wages, signing bonuses, tax-free and taxable benefits — all of the new cash flow available for investment must be discussed with your advisor when a new job is landed. This topic is discussed in detail in Chapter 7.

Starting a New Business
Lucrative tax deductions are available to those who begin a small business. In fact, in the start-up year, business losses could offset all other income of the current year or could be applied, if unused, to income of the prior three years. For this reason, the exit from current employment, severance package planning and investment planning surrounding the new venture must be carefully discussed with advisors. This topic is discussed in detail in Chapter 9.

IT WILL ALL PAY OFF
Tap the potential tax savings around milestones and life events by asking intelligent and pointed questions of your tax advisor before the event, if possible. Advisor Check-In 5.2 gives you a number of questions to review with your advisor for each event. Careful planning could save you thousands of dollars over time.

TAX PRO COACH
Your Strategic Plan for the Analysis of the Tax Consequences of Life Events
Events in your life and your family's have tax consequences that can influence current and future tax savings and planning. Be sure to discuss them with your advisor in advance of their occurrence, if possible. Discuss the following surrounding family milestones with your advisor:
- Can I consult with my advisor on a year-round basis and is it included in his tax preparation fee? If not, what would this service cost?

- How will my family respond to key life events and milestones and what are the tax consequences of these responses?
- Do my advisor and I agree on what life events are most significant to my tax planning affairs and when to trigger a meeting to discuss them?
- Ask my advisor to work with my other professional advisors to plan gift-giving during my lifetime and at death or when family members receive an inheritance or plan a will.
- Find out the tax consequences of life altering events like family moves, job termination or career change, divorce and emigration well before the parties are immersed in the life change itself.

While the discussions in Chapters 1 to 5 encompassed guidelines surrounding the basic relationship and information exchange required between taxpayers and their financial advisors, you will find the next five chapters zero in on the specific tax filing profiles most taxpayers fall into: caregivers, employees, investors, small business owners and executors. It is important to discuss the details of the special tax provisions of those who fall within these profiles with your advisor to ensure that decisions you make throughout the year encompass the after-tax benefits our tax system provides especially for these profiles.

The final chapter in this book, At A Glance, provides 30 of the most commonly overlooked tax saving opportunities to discuss with your advisors. Each provision is described in three ways: what you need to know, what documents you need to bring and what questions you need to ask. I hope you find this chapter especially useful in isolating, with your advisors, every tax benefit you are entitled to.

Advisor Check-In 5.1
Understanding Significant Milestones for You and Your Family

MILESTONE	QUESTIONS TO ASK
Birth to Age 6	• When does a tax return have to be filed for children of this age?
	• What are the tax consequences of transferring money or assets to minor children?
	• What are the tax consequences of hiring children in the family business?
	• How do I set up an informal or formal, yet CCRA-acceptable, trust fund for investment purposes?
	• How can I best use and invest the Canada Child Tax Benefit (CCTB) and other provincial tax credits received for this child?
	• What are the details of Registered Education Savings Plan (RESP) and other educational savings opportunities?
	• How is income of their own source reported?
	• Can Registered Retirement Savings Plan (RRSP) room be developed?
	• How can child care expenses be best claimed for the children and their activities?
	• What non-refundable tax credits do these children qualify for?
	• How can supporting individuals maximize claims for these children?
Age 7–16	• How do I claim child care expenses for children in this age group?
	• Will their day camps and other social or sporting activities qualify for child care?
	• Will their music or sports lessons qualify for a deduction?
	• How is the CCTB impacted by the claim for child care expenses?
	• Are there any special rules for claiming care costs if my child is disabled?
	• When can children file their own returns to claim refundable provincial or federal credits?
Age 17 & 18	• Should my child file a return to report his own income?
	• Who should claim the child's tuition and education amounts for university?
	• How should RESP income be reported?
	• Are board and lodging costs paid to attend a university out of town deductible?
	• Are moving expenses of a student deductible?
	• How are scholarships received from a foreign university taxed?
Age 19	• What are the tax consequences of supporting an adult child?
	• How is income-splitting affected when a child becomes an adult?
Age 20–29	• What are the tax consequences of marriage?
	• What are the tax consequences of divorce?
	• How is my return impacted when I live common law with my partner?
	• How should I negotiate my employment contract?
	• How much should I contribute to my RRSP each year?
	• How should I spend my extra savings — by paying off the mortgage or contributing to the RRSP?
	• What are the tax consequences of each of the types of investment earnings I can make?

- Should my spouse work or stay at home with the kids?
- What is the tax consequence of working, when we take into account the cost of transportation, clothes, babysitting, and other costs?
- What medical expenses are deductible to the family and who should claim them?
- Do we have adequate insurance coverage to build the kind of tax-free estate we want to leave?
- Who is writing off the safety deposit box?
- Are the costs of building a family cottage tax deductible?

Age 30 to 59	• How are capital gains and losses on the purchase, sale or transfer of assets treated for tax purposes?
	• How are disability benefits — from public or private plans — taxed?
	• What is the tax effect of receiving Employment Insurance?
	• How do lump sums received during the tax year effect my taxable income?
	• What is the best way to split income and pension accumulations with my spouse?
	• Should I leverage the equity in my home to take an investment loan?
	• What are the tax advantages of opening a small business?
	• How should my income be structured in retirement?
Age 60 plus	• Are income sources and tax brackets between spouses similar?
	• Who should withdraw taxable funds from registered accounts to gain the best tax advantage?
	• When should I tap into my Canada Pension Plan (CPP) pension and should I split the benefits with my spouse?
	• At what income level will my age amount and Old Age Security (OAS) be subject to clawback?
	• How can I withdraw funds (capital and earnings) from my non-registered funds more tax-advantageously?
	• What will the tax consequences of asset valuations be upon my death?
	• Would an estate freeze of the value of my shares in my small business corporation make sense?
	• How are the costs of medical treatments, devices and home care written off?
	• How can income be structured to minimize user fees for required services of the elderly?
	• What are the tax consequences upon receipt and investment of inherited property?

Advisor Check-In 5.2
Questions to Consider When You Encounter Key Life Events

WHEN ILLNESS OR DISABILITY STRIKES

- What claims can be made for the care of my child, who is disabled, while I work?
- How are lump-sum disability payments taxed and when?
- Is Registered Retirement Savings Plan (RRSP) earned income created on any of my disability income sources?
- How will withdrawals from an RRSP be taxed in this year and when should they be made?
- Can I reduce my taxable wage loss replacement benefits with any deductions?
- Will our home modification costs be deductible?
- What medical expenditures can be claimed?
- How do new income levels affect our claims for refundable and non-refundable credits?
- How can income be structured to reduce rates paid at nursing homes for my parent with disabilities?

SEPARATION OR DIVORCE

- Is there an advantageous time, from a tax viewpoint, to set a date of separation?
- How will each person's income levels be affected by the separation?
- Is it more advantageous to settle for a lump-sum or periodic payments?
- Who is responsible for tax payments to CCRA and what are the consequences of non-payment?
- What moving expenses can be deducted if one party moves out of province or out of the country?
- Does the taxation of support differ if it is received from a payor resident in the US?
- How is each party's RRSP contribution room affected by separation or divorce?
- Who will claim child care expenses and medical expenses for the family?
- How will retirement income be structured in the future to take advantage of each party's public and private income sources?
- How can asset transfers be maximized to use up prior losses or set adjusted cost base values that will be of most benefit now and when assets are actually sold in the future?
- What difference will each person's new income level make to the level of refundable tax credits available to each? Who will claim these credits?
- When and how should CCRA be notified of the change in status to adjust refundable tax credits and record changes in address, direct deposit accounts, etc.?
- What non-refundable tax credits does each party qualify for?
- Can legal fees be deducted on the cost of the separation or divorce or enforcement of payments?

WHEN LIFE ENDS

- What information is required to be left for my executor so that she can meet all obligations surrounding my final returns?
- What tax filing deadlines do I or my executors have to be aware of?
- How will the directives in my will affect my final tax return and that of my spouse and children?
- How are my assets valued when I die and what is the most tax-efficient way to handle their transfer to my beneficiaries?

- If I decide to gift money or assets during my lifetime, what are the tax consequences?
- How does the capital gains election I made in 1994 on my assets affect the taxes on my final return?
- How can I maximize my charitable donations?
- How will my interest and pension income sources be taxed at death and thereafter?
- How will my remaining RRSP room be used up in the event of my death?
- How should registered fund accumulations be distributed to beneficiaries?
- How will my various carry-overs be handled at my death, including unused capital and non-capital losses, unused past service contributions to company pension plans?
- What happens to required Lifelong Learning Plan or Home Buyers' Plan repayments at death?
- Should my assets and income streams flow through a family or testamentary trust?
- What are the special tax rules for claiming of dependants and other non-refundable tax credits in the year of death?
- Will funeral expenses be tax deductible?
- How can the expenses of infirmity before death affect family tax filing?
- What are the rules and options for payment of taxes owing upon death?

EARLY RETIREMENT OR SEVERANCE

- Will the receipt of severance from my employer bump me into a higher tax bracket?
- Can my taxes be reduced by taking severance over two taxation years or using an RRSP roll-over?
- Is it to my advantage to use my unused RRSP contribution room with my severance income?
- How do the changes in our family income affect our eligibility for refundable tax credits like the Canada Child Tax Benefit?
- How can I protect my Employment Insurance benefits from clawbacks on the tax return?
- Are the legal fees I paid to collect my severance package tax deductible?
- Are there other tax credits, such as Labour-Sponsored Investment Funds tax credits, which may help decrease tax liabilities?
- Are there transferable provisions we should be revisiting on our family tax returns?

GIFTS AND GIFT-GIVING

- Will there be a capital gain or loss on the deemed disposition that occurs upon transfer of the property during my lifetime?
- What valuation documents are required to enable the transfer of assets during my lifetime?
- To whom will income, resulting from the transferred asset, be taxed after the transfer?
- Are there special rules for the transfer of the family residences or family heirlooms to a spouse or children?
- What are the special rules surrounding the transfer of the family farm to another generation?
- Will I be eligible to claim the $500,000 capital gains exemption when I transfer assets to family members?
- What are the rules for donating gifts in kind or in donating publicly traded shares to charity?
- Can a life insurance policy be donated to charity and how must this be structured?

CHAPTER 6

Tax Strategies for Caregivers

- Understand how the tax system supports the caregiver
- Plan child and elder care spending from a tax-wise position
- Have a financial strategy established in case illness, accident or when special need strikes

Caregivers in our society today are an undervalued lot and most of us will be among them over the next decade or two. This chapter will help you think about this situation and discuss with your advisors the tax and financial implications of a future that may include caregiving.

It can be emotionally and physically exhausting to provide care to the very small, the elderly, sick or disabled. If you have ever spent nights awake nursing a feverish baby or days rushing to the side of your cancer-stricken parent, you are well aware of the personal and financial strain caregivers bear, while attempting to juggle a normally stressful life. It is an understatement to say that work-life balances can suffer and that caregiving will come with added financial burdens. Fortunately, there may be relief for the latter through the tax system.

For example, the decisions you may be required to make surrounding the care of your elderly parents may be particularly heart-wrenching. You may find yourself having to move your aging mother into a long-term care facility. In that case, the structure of your mother's retirement income can have a significant bearing on the per diem rate that must be paid to the home. It is important to understand this many years in advance, so that investment decisions or the plan to gift assets can be formulated with a view to reducing both realized income and personal care home costs.

In another instance, you may wish to move granny into your home to provide care yourself. However, before you can do so, home renovations must be completed to accommodate a wheelchair and special railings throughout the house. These costs may be tax deductible as medical expenses.

It is clear that the demands of caregiving for the elderly are an emerging issue that requires attention, not only from a social viewpoint as it relates to our health care system and other social services, but also from the point of view of the individual taxpayer.

Today, for example, we have approximately 22 million tax filers in Canada, out of a population of about 31 million. In ten years, it is estimated that about 15% of our population will be over the age of 60, and that over a million will be disabled. Hundreds of thousands of people will require community assistance, institutional care or care from their families.

Also, if you are a working person today and likely to be moving into a caregiving role sometime in the next ten years or so, you will require financial, emotional and physical resources to help you prepare for that burden. Now is the time to give your future some serious thought and to ensure you've planned well for your financial resources and personal health in that time.

Fortunately, there are a number of tax preferences that can be tapped to provide a small amount of compensation for the hardships of support and advocacy to others. As introduced in Chapter 3, at tax filing time a series of deductions, refundable and non-refundable tax credits are available for the family and those relating to caregiving expenses should be explored in depth with your tax advisor.

It is a fact that most families under the stress of caregiving make many errors and omissions in filing their own tax returns. (Figure 6.1 reviews many of these errors.) For this reason you may wish to seek the help of a tax professional, if you have not done so in the past. Ask her to review prior-filed returns for any errors or omissions that might be recovered.

If you have missed any of these provisions, or made errors claiming them, be sure to see a tax advisor about recovery of missed provisions. You can go all the way back to 1985 to do so, in most cases. Ask your tax advisor to do this for you.

Figure 6.1

Common Errors Made by Caregivers or Taxpayers who are Disabled

Income Sources

- Tax-exempt wage loss replacement benefits are added to income
- Taxable wage loss replacement benefits are not reduced by premiums paid
- Canada Pension Plan (CPP) orphan's benefits are added to the income of the surviving parent rather than the recipient child
- Employment Insurance (EI) benefits are eroded due to net income clawbacks
- Registered Retirement Savings Plan (RRSP) savings are cashed and bump taxpayers into higher tax brackets

Deductions

- Child care expenses are under-claimed or claimed by the wrong parent
- Parents are unaware of the $10,000 maximum claim allowed for children who are disabled
- Attendant care costs of up to $15,000 a year can be deducted when help is hired for a person who is disabled to go back to school or work

Non-Refundable Tax Credits

- Spousal or equivalent-to-spouse amounts are under-claimed because net income of the dependant is incorrect
- Amounts for infirm adult dependants, caregiver amount, disability amount and medical expenses are missed or under-claimed

Refundable Tax Credits

- The Canada Child Tax Benefit (CCTB), the Goods and Services Tax/Harmonized Sales Tax Credit (GST/HST Credit) and certain provincial refundable tax credits are reduced or eliminated because clawback zones interfere

Other Tax Credits

- Political contributions, Labour-Sponsored Venture Capital Tax Credits are underused or not filed on the right tax return

KEY TAX ISSUES FOR YOUR ADVISOR

People often think that tax planning is for the rich. In fact, it is average Canadian families who are in danger of paying the highest marginal taxes. Why? Because of clawbacks — a term we introduced in Chapter 3.

Clawbacks refer to the erosion of certain tax benefits the government distributes to low- and middle-income earners. That's generally people with incomes up to $60,000. Clawbacks of benefits like Old Age Security (OAS), Employment Insurance (EI) or Canada Child Tax Benefits (CCTB) occur when income falls between $20,000 and $60,000. It all depends, however, on how many children you have, in the case of the CCTB, and your combined family net income.

In short, the tax system does more than just collect taxes. It also redistributes income to Canadian families at low- and middle-income levels. However, the income reported and assessed in the spring of this year — last year's income — will be the means test for a host of different provisions you may or may not qualify for or qualify for in part. This includes the refundable and non-refundable tax credits listed above. When your income falls into clawback zones, your marginal tax rate sky-rockets, often to levels higher than those paid by the highest income earners. (For more information see *Tax Secrets for Tough Times*, by Evelyn Jacks.)

Herein lies the success of the communications strategies with your tax and financial advisors. If you plan your income structure and help yourself to the numerous tax deductions and credits you may be entitled to within the family, more of that income redistribution can be yours.

Canadians pay a lot of taxes when times are good. Fortunately, tough times are usually temporary. But if you are facing tough times, or even better, before they arise, be sure to see your tax advisor so that you arrange your affairs to pay the least taxes — and reap the most benefits from the tax system — when you most need them. The following events could trigger tough times:

• wage loss due to your own disability or illness
• birth of a child
• dependency of a child, parent, sibling or spouse
• death of a family member.

In light of these events, you also should ask how the following key issues should be dealt with:

• What effect does my Registered Retirement Savings Plan (RRSP) deduction have on the deductions and credits available to me when I care for others?
• Who should claim child care expenses when one spouse is disabled?

- How are refundable tax credits affected by disability or dependency in the family?
- How can I recover the costs of care provided in my home to adults who are disabled?
- Can the costs of home modifications, nursing home care or respite care be deducted?
- What types of disabilities qualify for the claiming of the disability amount?
- Can I claim missed medical expenses for health care premiums and other prescriptions or services?

The tax return is also the key financial instrument for managing a variety of other sources of income and societal support vital to the sick and disabled, so be sure to file every year or allow your tax pro to act as your advocate in filing a return for the purposes of determining:
- federal guaranteed income supplements
- the GST/HST credit
- provincial coverage for drugs (net income levels may determine deductibles
- personal care home costs (next income levels may determine per diem rates)
- costs of subsidized child care.

FOCUS ON INCOME CONTINUATION

Find out while you are healthy how you can put emergency savings into place to tide your family over when illness strikes. Do you have enough life insurance? Do you have critical illness insurance? How can you insure against wage loss when you are sick or when you have to take time off to care for others? How do public and private income sources interact to provide maximum benefits? Make sure you ask your advisor about the tax consequences of the investments you make into income continuation — before paying premiums and collecting benefits if possible. Ask your advisor about the tax consequences of generating income from the following:
- benefits from CPP
- benefits from employer-sponsored health and wage loss replacement plans
- benefits from privately-funded health insurance and income replacement plans
- benefits under EI
- income replacement using registered and non-registered savings
- income replacement with shareholders loans.

FOCUS ON DEDUCTIONS

There are really only three key tax deductions to focus in on with this family profile:

1. family RRSP deductions
2. child care expenses
3. attendant care expenses.

The Financial Vitality of the RRSP Expands

We have mentioned in earlier pages that one of the most important assets the tax system bestows upon Canadians is RRSP contribution room. Unfortunately, the vast majority of Canadians ignore their rights to use it. Only about 10% of us fully maximize contributions to an RRSP every year.

Despite the obvious — lost tax savings from the missed RRSP deduction and income deferral — there is another very important reason to get on top of your RRSP planning. Canadians who run into bad luck due to disability or the need to leave the workforce to care for others will miss out on the redistribution of income through our social safety net ... something that is based on the size of our net income as shown on the tax return.

Make sure that for the current tax year, all persons in the family who work maximize their RRSP contributions which will be based on last year's earned income. Ask your tax advisor to confirm that contribution figure for you. This is important, as next year, your income picture could be substantially different and your accumulated RRSP savings may, in fact, need to be tapped. So, get all your tax advantages from the RRSP deduction now and position yourself for the unexpected.

There are other reasons to be vigilant about your tax filing and RRSP contribution habits. When income fluctuates downward because of illness or the need to give care, the social safety net can kick in ... but only for those who file tax returns and whose net income levels do not exceed clawback zones. How can you reduce net income to increase those social benefits?

This is where a well-timed RRSP contribution can come in handy. RRSP deductions (for the high-income earner and the lower-earning family members) can increase eligibility for social benefits like EI and refundable benefits like the CCTB.

The moral? Always maximize your RRSP contribution room, even if you choose not to take your tax deduction until a year in which income is higher. Speak to your tax advisor about those options now so that when the storms of life move in, you will be prepared to ride them out.

Child Care and Attendant Care Deductions

There are two deductions used to reduce net income — the figure upon which your refundable tax credits will be based.

The first, child care expenses, has often been the centre of controversy. There are perceived tax benefits for working families who claim child care expenses as a deduction, when compared to the tax results of a family in which one earner supports a stay-at-home parent with children. In fact, when you look at net cash flow, after the expense of the child care is actually paid, the difference in taxation, if any, usually is due to a completely different reason. The family with two earners making the same income as the family with one often pays less tax because each person falls into a lower tax bracket than the sole high-income earner.

So, when deciding whether to go back to work or to quit work to take on a caregiving role, it is most important to understand the tax dynamics. Ask your tax professional to prepare several "what if" scenarios for you:

- What if I stopped working to look after my small children; thereby saving the child care expenses?
- What if I stopped working to look after my gravely ill mother?
- What if I went back to work, leaving my child or parent with disabilities in institutional care?
- What if I brought a paid attendant in to help me cope?
- What if I quit work to start a consulting business out of my home to better cope with the demands of my family members?
- What if my health fails too? Will my investments carry me through?

Your tax advisor can help you find the answers, perhaps in conjunction with other financial advisors. In particular, she'll outline the tax benefits available when you find yourself in a caregiving role. With an understanding of the tax consequences, the financial outcomes can be fully evaluated and you will be in a better position to make important personal choices. For example, if you want to spend the last year of your cancer-stricken mother's life with her or the first year of your newborn's life with him, can you do so without risking financial ruin?

Your goal is to use your professional relationships to help you assess the net bottom line — after tax, social benefits and all other costs are determined. Only then can important decisions about lifestyle be made in a fully informed manner.

Advisor Check-In 6.1 at the end of this chapter provides a number of questions you can ask your tax pro to gain a clearer understanding of the deductions available and whether they can be applied to you and your family members' tax filing profiles.

FOCUS ON NON-REFUNDABLE TAX CREDITS

There are several key tax preferences that can reduce your tax burden if you are a caregiver, provided that you have taxable income. There are fewer factors to consider if you are alone, at a low income level and stricken yourself. See Check-In 6.2 for a guide to non-refundable credits for caregivers.

FOCUS ON REFUNDABLE TAX CREDITS

In Chapter 3 we outlined the levels of federal refundable tax credits: CCTB and the GST/HST Credit. Ask your tax advisor about provincial tax credits that may be available to you as well. But most important, know that if you don't file a tax return, you can't receive these benefits, so do so even if you don't have income. If you are a senior who is not mobile, ask for at-home service from your tax pro.

FOCUS ON INVESTMENTS

We have spoken about the importance of the RRSP in the determination of net income and the size of refundable tax credits, under Focus on Deductions, above. A tax focus on other non-registered investments is also critical for families dealing with caregiving issues.

Make no mistake, *income structure matters*. It is very important to speak with your tax and financial advisors many years before retirement or illness about income structure in times of sickness or in preparation for older age. For example, growth in the investments in life insurance policies or appreciating assets will not impact net income, while interest, Registered Retirement Investment Fund (RRIF) withdrawals and dividends will. Proper investment tax planning can help preserve your estate if your destiny is to spend years in a nursing home. Personal tax planning will help you maximize benefits available under a tax system set up to help the less fortunate.

TAX PRO COACH
Your Strategic Plan to Tax Savings for Canadian Families
Who Provide Care

Manage your future carefully by discussing income structure and tax preferences available to caregivers and their dependants. Discuss the following
questions with your advisor:

- How are my potential caregiver responsibilities for the young or the
  elderly going to impact me and my family members in the future from
  both a tax and financial planning viewpoint?
- What specific tax provisions will my family qualify for when there are new
  expenditures for child or elder care?
- How do the results of my elderly parent's tax return impact fees payable
  for drugs or personal care home fees?
- What are the financial consequences of in-home care versus private or
  institutional care out of the home and how are the tax returns of the
  family members affected by these options? Have we discussed "what if"
  scenarios to determine the net financial consequences?
- What would happen to my family's financial situation from a tax perspective if I became ill or had to take substantial time off to care for an aging
  parent?

Advisor Check-In 6.1
Guide to Discussion About Child Care Deductions

1. WHO IS ELIGIBLE TO CLAIM CHILD CARE EXPENSES?

Child care expenses may be claimed by parents who must pay another individual to care for their children so that they may earn income from employment or self-employment or so that they may attend school either full- or part-time. Paying for child care to do volunteer work or look after a sick parent will not be allowed. There must be earned income sources. Ask your tax pro to help you define your eligibility for this claim.

2. WHO QUALIFIES AS AN ELIGIBLE DEPENDANT?

Expenses are deductible for the care of dependant children who were under the age of 16 (at any time during the year) or who are physically or mentally infirm. An eligible child must be your child, your spouse or common-law partner's child or a child who was dependent on you or your spouse (or partner). If the child is not your child or your spouse's or partner's child, the child's net income must be less than the basic personal amount. Your tax pro can help you determine which dependants will qualify.

3. WHEN CAN I DEDUCT BABYSITTING EXPENSES?

Usually the money you actually paid to a Canadian resident is deductible if you have a receipt to prove it. Babysitters may be related to you, but if they are, the sitter must be over age 17. Payments made to a parent of the child or to a supporting person are not deductible. Your tax pro will ask you to provide the receipts which should have your sitter's Social Insurance Number on it.

4. WHAT IS EARNED INCOME FOR THE PURPOSE OF THIS DEDUCTION?

The child care deduction is limited to two-thirds of earned income. Earned income includes
- salaries and wages
- net profits from self-employment
- training allowances, the taxable portion of scholarships, bursaries, fellowships and research grants
- disability pensions under Canada (or Quebec) Pension Plan

5. ARE THERE ANY SPECIAL RULES AROUND CHILD CARE EXPENSE CLAIMS FOR STUDENTS?

Ask your tax pro to tell you more about the child care expense claim allowed to full- and part-time students with children.

6. CAN I CLAIM CHILD CARE EXPENSES IF I EARN A RELATIVELY HIGH INCOME?

Generally, child care expense claims may only be claimed by the lower income spouse (or partner). The lower income spouse is the one whose net income, before claiming child care expenses, is the lowest. But it is possible that the higher income spouse may claim child care expenses if the other spouse was a student or incapable of caring for the child because of mental or physical infirmity or was confined to a prison or similar institution for at least two weeks.

Advisor Check-In 6.2
Guide to Discussion of Non-Refundable Credits for Caregivers

FOR THOSE WHO LIVE ALONE

Your tax advisor will ensure you claim the full benefits of:

- the age amount (for those age 65 and older)
- the pension income amount (for those who receive private pension income)
- the disability amount
- medical expenses
- medical expenses supplement (only if there is earned income from employment or self-employment).

FOR THOSE WHO CARE FOR A SPOUSE OR COMMON-LAW PARTNER

If you are providing care to your sick spouse, your tax advisor will be claiming the following credits and asking you for income information from your spouse, as well as all the receipts the family has to support claims:

- an increased spousal amount
- a transfer of the spouse's age, disability, pension or tuition and education amounts
- of medical expenses and charitable donations
- of the medical expense supplement — but only if there is income from employment or self-employment sources.

FOR THOSE WHO CARE FOR OTHER RELATIVES

If you are providing care to other relatives who are sick, your advisor will be claiming the following credits and asking you for supporting documents:

- the amount for infirm dependants age 18 and older
- the caregiver amount
- the claiming of medical expenses for that dependant.

WHAT YOUR ADVISOR NEEDS TO CLAIM THE DISABILITY AMOUNT

Form T2201, Disability Tax Credit Certificate, must be signed by the patient's doctor. Ask your tax pro for this form.

ADULTS

In order to qualify for the disability amount, an adult taxpayer must meet the following criteria:

- Can the patient perform the basic activities of daily living: walking, speaking, perceiving, thinking, remembering, hearing, feeding, dressing, eliminating body waste?
- Is the patient "markedly restricted" — unable to perform basic activities of daily living even with therapy and the use of appropriate devices and medication?
- Is the impairment expected to last for a continuous period of at least 12 months?
- Must the patient take life sustaining therapy at least three times per week lasting an average of at least 14 hours per week? This includes clapping therapy to help with breathing or kidney dialysis.

CHILDREN

In order to qualify for the disability amount, a child must meet the following criteria:

- The child is blind.
- The child needs life sustaining therapy.
- The child's development progress is impaired.
  - From birth to age three, the child's developmental progress is assessed in comparison to the norm.
  - After the age of three, it is assessed by how the impairment affects the child's ability to perform the basic activities of daily living.

THE CREDIT FOR INFIRM ADULTS AGE 18 OR OLDER

This amount can be claimed by a supporting individual caring for an adult dependant other than your spouse: adult children, grandchildren, parents, grandparents, brothers, sisters, aunts, uncles, nephews or nieces, including in-laws. These relatives must be living in Canada and the credit is reduced by their net income levels. You must provide your advisor with their net income. Also discuss the following with your advisor:

- How much income can my dependant make before it affects my claim?
- If my dependant has unused claims, can they be transferred to my return?
- Just how "infirm" does a dependant have to be to qualify for this amount?
- Can more than one person make this claim for the same dependant?
- Can I make any other claims for the same dependant?

THE CAREGIVER AMOUNT

Since 1998, Canadian families have been able to claim an additional credit that allows for a higher net income earnings level in calculating the claim for an adult who is disabled and being cared for in the home. Originally the provision was meant for those who care for their parents or grandparents who are 65 years of age or older. However, this credit can now be claimed by those who care for the same list of relatives as described above under infirm adults age 18 or older. Only one of the two credits is claimable for the same dependant, however. This credit is for home care. The dependant must live with the caregiver in a home provided by the caregiver.

CHAPTER 7

Tax Tips for Employees and Executives

- Increase your employment tax efficiency
- Negotiate for both cash and benefits
- Avoid tax refunds by managing tax withholdings at source
- Be aware of deductible employment expenses
- Find ways to accumulate more wealth while working for your employer

Not making enough money? No raise in sight? Whether you work in the mailroom or the boardroom, you may be surprised to learn how easy it is to increase your take-home pay significantly with a little savvy tax planning.

Did you know that most employees overpay their taxes throughout the year — by a considerable sum? The statistics tell us that by April 30, 2001, CCRA had processed 7.1 million or one-third of the tax returns that would be filed that year. On those returns, refunds totalling $7.7 billion were processed with the average amount being $1,082.48. This is too large a number to be taken out of your family's budget every year and there is something you can do about that, as you'll learn in this chapter.

Refunds occur because the employer makes source deductions on the employee's behalf based on a screening process that does not take into account all personal tax provisions. That's why so many people end up with a tax refund — and that's simply not tax efficient. Your preference is, of course, to pay only the correct amount of tax all year long and not one cent more — leaving more in your pocket for wealth creation and more fun.

Consider this. If you worked for 35 years as an employee and had a tax refund of $1,000 each year, that would be $35,000 of potential investment power lost. If you always treated your tax refund as new investment capital, that potential would translate into even more. At a 5% annual rate of return, that $1,000 per year would grow to over $65,500, after taxes, after 35 years. You would see even more dramatic results if you invested that same $1,000 within your Registered Retirement Savings Plan (RRSP), turning that $1,000 annual investment into over $140,000 after 35 years. (Taxes must still be paid on withdrawal of your RRSP accumulations, but you should be able to see an important concept by comparing these numbers: savings within an RRSP grow significantly due to the deferral of taxes on the income earned and the reinvestment of the tax savings that result from an RRSP contribution every year.) Therefore, you should challenge your tax advisor to help you structure your affairs to break even at tax time so that you can always leverage your productivity and that of your money.

The overpayment of tax withholding at source is not the only serious error made by employed taxpayers. Others include the failure to claim allowable out-of-pocket expenses of employment, including income-splitting with family members, missing the Goods and Services Tax/Harmonized Sales Tax (GST/HST) rebate on those expenses and under-claiming medical expenses and charitable donations.

Time is money, and now is the best time to work with your tax pro to help you maximize your tax advantages.

KEY TAX ISSUES FOR YOUR ADVISOR

It's your job to ensure you file your return by April 30, but it's up to your tax pro to discuss with you the tax savings strategies common to an employment tax filing profile. This could include:

- reporting of various employment income sources and deductions, offset appropriately by personal credits
- creation and savvy use of RRSP contribution room
- claiming unique deductions like the cost of supplies, assistants, sales and promotion expenses, travel, home office, auto expenses, moving expenses not reimbursed, employee home relocation loan deductions, employee stock option and shares deductions
- recovery of medical expenses or charitable donations not otherwise reimbursed
- the vigilant review of prior-filed returns to ensure all tax preferences were claimed in prior years too

Because employees are in a master-servant relationship, it is expected that the employer will be taking all the risks, supplying the assets and paying salaries regardless of the financial health of the company. Therefore, employees are allowed very few deductions from their employment income.

On the other hand if you are an employee, you're at very low risk for audit. That's because CCRA will have already received a copy of the T4 Slip issued to you at the end of the year. This slip summarizes your earnings and your statutory source deductions: Canada Pension Plan (CPP), Employment Insurance (EI) and income tax. Tax filing is deceivingly simple.

Figure 7.1
Provisions that Can Reduce Income Tax Withholding

There are many taxes that you can request your employer withhold or reduce the amount of tax you pay before you pay. Consider the following categories with your advisor and stop providing the government with an interest-free loan.

- Registered Retirement Savings Plan (RRSP) contributions
- union and professional dues not paid on a payroll deduction plan
- child care expenses
- moving expenses
- allowable business investment losses
- employment expenses
- carrying charges including interest costs for investment loans
- repayments of social benefits like Employment Insurance (EI)
- deductible alimony or maintenance payments
- net business or rental losses
- loss carryovers (capital or non-capital)
- northern residents' deductions
- significant medical expenses or charitable donations
- overseas employment tax credits
- Labour-Sponsored Funds Tax Credits
- any other provisions that will reduce your taxable income.

However, once you understand your options, working with your advisor you can plan to avoid overpaying your taxes with every pay cheque and get the benefit of having your tax refund all year long.

To do so, explore the following key issues with your tax pro:

- **Tax Reporting:** Is withholding for income taxes, CPP and EI too high?
- **Focus on Income:** Can you diversify your employment earnings? Will your future pension accumulations be sufficient to fund the lifestyle you want in retirement?

- **Focus on Deductions:** What out-of-pocket expenses can be claimed?
- **Focus on Investments:** How can pension savings and wealth creation be increased?
- **Focus on Family:** Can your relationship with the employer help reduce the costs of health care, education, child care, recreation?

TAX REPORTING

Be sure to pay only the correct amount of tax, then invest the rest for your family's long-term gain. Otherwise you are giving the government an interest-free loan. Figure 7.1 lists the provisions that can reduce the amount of tax that your employer withholds. But also discuss the following with your tax advisor:

- **Don't Overpay — Get Help with Your TD1.** The level at which your income taxes are withheld is fixed when you complete Form TD1 (Personal Tax Credits Return) at the start of your employment and usually annually. Ask your tax pro to help you complete this form, based on your tax filing profile. If you still find you have a large tax refund at the end of the year, it means that you have many more deductions and credits than the form allows you to indicate and that you should take further action to reduce your tax withholding throughout the year.
- **Get Permission for Your Employer to Reduce Your Tax Withholding.** Ask your tax pro to complete Form T1213 (Request to Reduce Tax Deductions at Source) when you have your tax return prepared. Once this form is forwarded to CCRA, they will send a Letter of Authority to your employer, allowing the employer to reduce tax withholding. You'll have more money in your pocket throughout the year to be used for investment, retirement savings and cost-reduction.
- **Lots of T4s?** If you worked for more than one employer, it is possible you have overpaid your CPP and EI source deductions and could find increased tax refunds as a result the overpayments. You'll also have over-contributed if you turned 18, 70, or started receiving CPP retirement benefits during the year. Ask your tax pro to identify the amount of your CPP/EI overpayments. Then, always invest this money in your own safety-net — your RRSP or non-registered investment account.
- **Missed T4?** Contact your tax pro immediately if you receive a T4 Slip you have forgotten about. An adjustment will need to be made to your return — never file a second tax return for the same year.

Figure 7.2
Tax-Free and Taxable Benefits

Tax-Free Benefits	Taxable Benefits
• Athletic, recreation or social club memberships	• Personal use of an employer-provided vehicle
• Counselling services for mental or physical health or re-employment or retirement	• Financial counselling and income tax return preparation
• Discounts on merchandise in store	• Value of frequent flyer points earned while travelling on company business but used by the employee for personal travel
• Moving expenses, if move required by employer	
• Non-cash gifts up to $500 in value	
• Premiums paid for private health care plans	• One-half of any reimbursement (in excess of $15,000) for loss on the sale of a former residence when moving
• Remote or special worksites: board and lodging, subsidized school services, transportation to special site, reasonable costs of away-from-home education of employee's child	
• Subsidized meals in employer's caferia, etc.	• Value of gifts where the total value for the year exceeds $500
• Premiums under wage loss replacement plans	• Premiums under wage loss replacement plans
• Transportation passes of retired employees	• Free or subsidized board and lodging except at a remote or special worksite or while travelling away from the municipal area of the work location for more than 12 hours
• Uniforms, special clothes and dry cleaning costs	
• Education costs where training is primarily for the benefit of the employer	
• Employer's contribution to provincial hospitalization and medical care insurance plans	• Reimbursement for the cost of tools
• Professional membership fees where membership is a requirement of employment	• Travelling expenses for the employee and/or his family except for a reasonable allowance for travel expenses of a sales representative, reimbursement of employment expenses, or travel expenses for away-from-home education of a child of an employee living at a remote or special worksite
• Most disability related employment benefits such as transportation, parking, services of an attendant, readers for the blind, signers for the deaf or coaches for the intellectually impaired	
• Meals provided during occasional overtime	• Holiday trips, prizes and other incentive awards
	• Education costs where training is not primarily for the benefit of the employer
	• Employee's contribution to provincial hospitalization and medical care insurance plans if paid by the employer
	• Group life insurance premiums
	• Interest-free or low-interest loans
	• RRSP contributions made by the employer
	• Difference in value between exercise price and fair market value of exercised employee stock options

FOCUS ON INCOME

All taxable remuneration or benefits received by an employee are reported as received in a calendar year and there is almost no way to split the employment income with other family members. One exception concerns the hiring of an assistant, as discussed under Focus on Deductions later in this chapter. Also, it is possible for employees to earn tax-free employment perks, if they are in the know about the potential for tax-free benefits.

For example, your employer may require that you take certain courses of importance to the company or to entertain clients at a club preferred by your employer. When your employer pays for these things it's primarily for his benefit, so the amount is not taxed to you. In other cases, the employer may pay for items of benefit to you — your vacation or a car that is available for your personal as well as business use. In that case, the benefits become taxable to you.

Familiarize yourself with the benefits that are taxable and those that aren't in Figure 7.2. Then discuss with your advisor which benefits you should focus on in employment negotiations or at salary reviews.

Negotiate for Cash and Perks

Be sure to speak to your tax advisor about broadening your employment negotiations. Look for an employer who can offer both cash and perks, such as tax-free memberships to recreational clubs or the taxable use of an employer-provided vehicle. You may also wish to look for an employment contract that offers a stock option plan or a company that makes low-interest loans, as a way to diversify your income and build tax-deferred wealth.

It is important to enter your employment negotiations or annual performance reviews with some tax savvy. Whether you are renegotiating with an existing employer or looking at starting with a new company in which you will be hiring employees yourself, speak to your tax advisor about the different forms of employment remuneration and their tax consequences. Discuss some of the finer points of your employment agreements with your advisor using Advisor Check-In 7.1 at the end of the chapter.

Understand How Your Income is Taxed

Employment income is taxed at the highest marginal rates. To tax cost average (reduce your lifetime income tax bill over time), it's important to work with your tax and financial advisors to develop income sources outside of employment, either through the acquisition of ownership in the company through stock options or the ability to otherwise build up a diversified investment portfolio within registered pension plans and non-registered accounts. By ensuring that your employer's dollar provides for as many of your life needs as possible, you can accumulate more wealth.

Timing the receipt of additional remuneration is important. Before receiving bonuses and severance packages, ask your tax advisor to prepare several "what if" scenarios with the objective of choosing a tax-preferred time to take those income sources.

FOCUS ON DEDUCTIONS

As an employee your ability to write off expenses is limited, so you won't want to spend money on buying cell phones or computers, for example, if you can avoid it. CCRA considers that with the exception of automobile, aircraft or musical instruments used in the course of your employment, all capital assets required to do your work will be supplied by the employer. However, if you are required to supply your own equipment like a computer or cell phone, the cost of leasing the equipment is deductible. And there are still a number of expenses that you can write off under certain circumstances. Check the list below and discuss with your advisor how you can reduce your taxes with these legitimate expenses.

Salary Only

For employees who earn salary only, they may deduct the following out-of-pocket expenses, if not reimbursed by employer:

- accounting and legal fees, not including income tax preparation costs
- motor vehicle expenses including capital cost allowance, interest or leasing costs, as well as operating costs
- travelling expenses, including rail, air, bus or other travel costs
- meals, tips and hotel costs providing excursion is for at least 12 hours away from the taxpayer's metropolitan area (meals and tips are subject to a 50% restriction)
- costs of parking (but generally not at the place of employment)
- supplies used up directly in the work (stationery, maps, etc.)
- salaries paid to your assistant (including spouses or children if fair market value is paid for work actually performed)
- office rent or certain home office expenses described below.

Salary and Commission

For employees who earn their living negotiating contracts for their employers or selling on commission, if they are required to pay their own expenses and regularly perform their duties away from their employer's place

of business, expenses may be claimed. In addition, expenses are claimable only if the employee is not in receipt of a tax-free travel allowance. Deductible travel expenses include:
- automobile-related operating expenses like gas, oil, repairs
- automobile-related fixed costs like licenses, insurance, interest, leasing and capital cost allowance
- the cost of air, bus, rail, taxi or other transportation which takes the employee outside the employer's metropolitan terminal
- promotional expenses
- entertainment (subject to the 50% restriction)
- travel and auto
- home office.

Deductible Home Office Costs
Employed taxpayers may claim home office costs but are limited to the following if they earn salary only:
- rent
- utility costs
- cleaning materials and minor repairs for the office
- employed commission salespeople may add the costs of property taxes and insurance.

Note: Employees may never claim costs relating to mortgage interest or capital cost allowance.

Recovering Expenses
There are two ways to recover your out-of-pocket expenses of employment. The most direct route is to have the employer reimburse you for those expenses with every pay cheque. Don't let these costs accumulate on your credit cards as the high interest costs will not be deductible. So be vigilant about sorting and processing your out-of-pocket expenditures before each pay period cut-off.

Using the tax return as a route of reimbursement is less efficient. That's because you are paying these expenses with after-tax dollars and then waiting to reap tax relief many months later when you file your tax return. There is a better way to handle this. During the year, make sure your tax withholding levels are adjusted downward in cases where you are required, under your contract of employment, to pay out-of-pocket expenses yourself.

When making a claim for employment expenses, you will need to have your employer sign Form T2200 (Declaration of Conditions of Employment), in which he certifies that those expenditures are a requirement of your contract for employment. Without this signed form on hand in case of audit, your deductions of employment expenses will be denied. Ask your tax advisor to give you one to take to your employer at tax time.

Good News for Commission Sales People

Commission sales employees may take further action in reducing their income tax source withholdings by filing Form TD1X (Commission Income and Expenses for Payroll Tax Deductions). This will allow the employer to reduce income tax withheld at source when there are employment expenses to be claimed against commission income. Note that the commission sales people must have the employer sign Form T2200 (Declaration of Condi tions of Employment) in order to write off any employment expenses.

FOCUS ON INVESTMENTS

It is important for an employee to look for ways to diversify income and it is preferable if some of those opportunities emerge from the relationship with the employer. Advisor Check-In 7.2 offers some questions you can ask of your advisor to maximize investment opportunities through your employer.

One of the most important investments you can make, as an employee, is to shore up your retirement savings plans. Be sure you understand your employer's company pension plan, when you can participate, how much will be there when you are ready to tap into it and what your alternative savings routes can be.

Be sure to maximize your RRSP contribution room, if any is available. Then leverage this investment by speaking to your tax pro about other tax credits you can easily access, like the Labour-Sponsored Funds Tax Credit. You don't have to come up with any new money, simply choose to put funds within the RRSP into a Labour-Sponsored Investment Fund to reap a tax credit of 15% federally and another 15% or more provincially, where available. The merits of this investment, like all other investment decisions, should however be based on its fit within your overall financial plan.

FOCUS ON FAMILY

Employers often make it easy for families to have their basic needs met by offering the following benefits of employment (be sure you include these in your "wish list" for your next employment contract negotiation):

- Group health, dental and drug plans: Ask about the deductibility of your premiums and how any wage loss replacement benefits may be taxed in the future.
- Group insurance: Ask about the deductibility of your premiums.
- Education costs: If the courses are taken for your employer's benefit, the tuition fees paid by the employee will be tax free.
- Child care: Subsidized child care at the employer's work location is a tax-free benefit.
- Computers: Computers given to employees for the purposes of working out of their homes are a tax-free benefit.
- Recreation: Memberships to family fitness, recreation or social clubs are a tax-free benefit, if the memberships contribute to the employer's business.

Should the Spouse Go Back to Work?

There is one other issue that is often discussed with advisors in families where one spouse is considering new employment after going to school or staying home to look after children. Families often wonder whether it makes tax sense for the spouse to go back to work?

In fact, in cases where both spouses are primarily making income from employment, it is quite possible that the family with two earners could pay less tax than the family in which there is one earner making a higher wage, while his spouse stays home. This will depend on income levels and whether there are child care expenses.

Ask your tax advisor to compute the tax cost of two working spouses. Take into account:

- costs of lost spousal amount
- costs of babysitting (net of tax savings on child care expenses)
- costs of reduced CCTB
- ability to shore up retirement saving opportunities
- ability to split income and therefore reduce overall tax bill
- additional costs for others to perform work that would otherwise have been done by the non-working spouse
- additional costs of transportation and other employment-related expenses.

FOCUS ON "WHAT IF" SCENARIOS

It is important to remember that even as an employee there is much you can do to build wealth by managing the tax you pay. Developing a number of "what if" scenarios with your tax pro will provide you with an understanding of what actions and decisions will impact your taxes and provide you with a frame of reference for future decisions. Start with some of these scenarios:

- accepting a signing bonus
- accepting a severance package
- receiving an employer-provided vehicle
- moving to another city or province
- enhancing education through your employment
- receiving counselling for retirement or re-employment
- maximizing your retirement savings
- changing status from employee to sub-contractor
- moving from an employer-provided workplace to an office in the home
- hiring a family member as your assistant.

TAX PRO COACH
Your Strategic Plan for Tax Savings for Employees in the Family

Focus on minimizing the government's tax bite out of your periodic pay cheque throughout the year so that you can get the benefits of investing your tax-efficient dollar to your advantage all year. Those benefits are worth hundreds of thousands of dollars to you over your lifetime. Ask your advisor to quantify this for you by projecting the value of your tax refund into the future, under several investment options including the purchase of both registered and non-registered investments.

Find direction with specific questions for your tax advisor:

- How can I reduce the size of my tax refund at the end of the year to better use my money throughout the year?
- What out-of-pocket expenses that I incur on behalf of my employment activities are deductible and what paperwork is required to stay onside with CCRA?
- Do my advisor and I agree on where I should focus my energies during my annual salary negotiation?
- What tax implications should I be aware of if I plan to switch jobs (e.g. salary, benefits, pension planning)?
- What are the tax implications I need to know about in case I lose my job or decide to retire early?

Advisor Check-In 7.1

Questions to Ask About Employment Negotiations

Contact your tax pro early to discuss the tax implications of certain negotiated benefits. Here are some questions you might start with.

- **Signing bonus:** Should I ask for cash or for stock options?
- **Auto:** What are the tax implications of receiving an employer-owned versus employer-leased vehicle to use?
  - What is my cash flow after the tax deductions for the value of the vehicle?
  - Who is covering the expenses of the vehicle?
  - When is the tax cost of the vehicle too expensive for its age and model?
  - What are the tax implications if I buy the car off lease?
- **Club memberships:** Is a membership to the local athletic club a tax-free benefit?
- **Death benefits:** Can I ask for a tax-free benefit of up to $10,000 in case of my death while working?
- **Group health benefits:** Are long-term disability benefits taxable to me when I collect them? Are premiums for health care insurance deductible as a medical expense?
- **Home office:** If my employer requires me to work out of my home, what part of the workspace can I claim? Is it more tax-efficient for me if my employer supplies the computer, Internet and communications costs?
- **Investment loans:** Are low-interest or interest-free loans to make investments in the company stock option plan taxable?
- **Meals and entertainment:** When I entertain clients on my employer's behalf, can I deduct the cost? How do I claim the cost of meals and lodging on the road if I take a job as a long distance transport driver?
- **Performance bonuses:** When should I receive my bonus: now or early in the new year?
- **Professional development:** Should I pay for my continuing education costs from savings, through my employer's investment in me or through withdrawals from my Registered Retirement Savings Plan (RRSP)?
- **Severance:** How much of my severance package will be offset with RRSP contribution opportunities?
- **Relocation:** How should I be compensated for relocation, if this is required by the employer? Talk to your tax pro about receiving:
  - Assistance for moving costs, sale of home, losses on sale of home
  - Temporary living costs at new location
  - Home relocation loan to help with new mortgage
  - Counselling or job placement assistance for spouse
  - Private school and private sporting program relocation allowances for children

Advisor Check-In 7.2
Employment Related Questions to Focus on Tax Savings

There are many opportunities to reap tax savings in the world of work. Here are some questions, sorted by topic, to get you started with your advisor.

INCOME RELATED

- Am I overpaying my taxes every pay period when my employer deducts taxes at source?
- What is the tax cost of my employer-provided vehicle? Can I reduce it?
- What taxable benefits have I received through my employment and do I qualify for any offsetting deductions?
- How can I incorporate more tax-free benefits into my employment agreement?
- Are the fees I receive for strike pay taxable? What documentation is required?
- How is my salary deferral arrangement taxed?
- When is the best time for me to take my employer's offer of a transfer to another province?
- What are the tax consequences of taking stock options as part of my employment agreement?
- Do I qualify for special tax benefits because I work at a remote worksite?
- As an employed musician, how can I write off the costs of maintaining my musical instrument?
- How will a non-competition agreement with my employer at the end of my term be taxed?
- How will my remuneration as director of the company be taxed?
- How is my travelling allowance reported on my tax return?

EMPLOYMENT RELATED

- Are the out-of-pocket expenses I pay as an employee tax deductible to me? What forms need to be filed?
- Can I claim the Christmas gifts I will give to my potential clients if I have no commission sales income until the next tax year?
- Can I deduct the taxable benefit I pay on the interest-free loan my employer gave me to buy company shares?
- Are my group health care premiums deductible and will wage loss replacement benefits be taxable to me if I become ill?

INVESTMENT AND PENSION RELATED

- What is my Registered Retirement Savings Plan (RRSP) contribution room and how much have I over- or under-contributed?
- How much of my past service contributions that I make to my employer's superannuation plan can be deducted on my tax return?
- How will the stock options my employer is offering to me be handled on my tax return?
- How can I maximize the use of my employer's money in my investment or home buying objectives?

- Should I purchase investments like RRSPs and Canada Savings Bonds through the payroll plan at work?
- How should death benefits left to my spouse when I die be structured to provide him with the best tax benefits?
- Should I buy life insurance through a group plan at work and what happens to that coverage if I leave my employer?
- What is the value of my company pension plan at age 55, 60, and 65?
- Will my health care premiums become part of my retirement plan when I leave my employer?

JOB CHANGE AND/OR TERMINATION

- What is the ideal form of remuneration I should be seeking — cash, benefits, stock options, etc.?
- What is the best way to handle my severance package to minimize tax?

CHAPTER 8

Tips for Tax-Efficient Investing

- ▥ **Bring focus to future tax and investment planning**
- ▥ **Understand the difference between income and capital**
- ▥ **Create income for four distinct purposes in life**
- ▥ **Utilize deductions and credits to enhance income**

There are few Canadians invested in equity markets who have not felt queasy about market volatility recently. Not only have we lost value in our retirement savings with market declines, but we have lost the value of an even more important asset. That asset is time.

To put this into context, think about how long it takes to double your money. Using the Rule of 72 (72 is divided by your rate of return) for example, you will find that at the average compound rate of Canada Premium Bonds (4.06%), it will take about 18 years to double your money. At 10% it takes 7.2 years. Given recent savings results, for many Canadians a lifetime of accumulated savings and debt have amounted to pre-retirement results that are somewhat short of their comfort zones.

The Need for a New Focus

There are some who would argue that ultimately, wealth accumulation is perpetual and that what's important is to grow a financial tree to bear fruit for generations to come. If that is so, current market conditions are likely irrelevant to most inter-generational accumulators.

The structure of capital or income withdrawals during a single retirement lifecycle can make or break that tree. Going forward, the prime motivation for investment planning — retirement savings — should perhaps have an entirely different focus. The need for your family financial tree to bear fruit at retirement must be carefully planned, but when the objective is to preserve the trunk, that need is a temporary one, in the scheme of things.

If investors can accept and embrace the concept of long-term financial planning to span past their own lifetimes, the feat of investment planning becomes much more interesting and the task of retirement income creation more focused on lifestyle objectives.

This is where tax planning comes in. The less tax you pay the more you have to live on and that factors prominently into planning for your financial tree to bear fruit for generations to come. Your goal in working with your tax advisors then is simple:

1. Identify sources of income and capital that will make up your retirement annuity.
2. Compute how these will be taxed.
3. Increase income with tax reduction strategies.
4. Develop a plan for the preservation of capital that will allow you to live your retirement years without the worry of depletion. That involves the peace of mind of knowing your estate plan is in place.

It is extremely significant, for example, that increases in the value of your principal residence constitute tax-exempt receipts, while accumulations in registered funds can continue to accrue tax sheltered growth well into retirement. Life insurance policies provide for sheltered income accumulations, an opportunity to create a tax-free pension by borrowing against the value of the policy and a tax-exempt remaining benefit for your estate at death.

In short, you have options for the creation of the future you envision for yourself and your heirs. The important thing to do today, together with your tax and financial advisors, is to focus forward.

KEY TAX ISSUES FOR YOUR ADVISOR

Focus is the result of purpose. The positive side of recent volatility in the stock markets is that new purpose has been created for investors and their advisors to come together and strategize the future.

There are several key issues to discuss immediately:

1. How much time is there between now and retirement?
2. How much income will we need upon retirement? For what purposes?
3. What is the asset mix that will allow us to generate those investment returns in the time frame we need them?
4. How much of our capital will that income requirement erode?

5. How can tax planning help us accumulate faster?
6. How can tax planning help us withdraw funds more efficiently?
7. How can tax planning help us to pass on as much capital as possible to future generations or for long life spans?
8. How much capital is required to fund our estate adequately?
9. How much capital is required to throw off income returns that will allow the family to survive periods of hardship, including unexpected illness or loss of work?
10. How can new capital be generated from overpaid taxes of the past?

Take the time to review these ten vital questions with your tax and financial advisory team. The answers will provide you with direction and solutions to act upon in your daily decision-making.

FOCUS ON INCOME

It is important for you to set more definitive life and financial plans if you find yourself worrying about stock market volatility or other factors that you think will affect your lifestyle. Seek the help of a financial planner immediately to focus on four distinct saving periods in your life:

1. **Current Needs:** How do I reduce the taxes on my income now to create new capital for investment, reduce my debt load and free up current income for other needs?
2. **Income in Retirement:** How do I create the income structure I will need in the future for retirement?
3. **Income for Education:** How do I create education savings for my children and grandchildren?
4. **Income for Me:** How do I fund the lifestyle I want to live and preserve my capital tree?

Create Tax-Efficient Income

There are several concepts you and your tax advisors should discuss in structuring income and savings plans on a tax-efficient basis to meet the goals above:

- Capital is not taxed, unless you withdraw money from a Registered Retirement Savings Plan (RRSP) or Registered Retirement Investment Fund (RRIF).
- Interest is taxed at higher marginal rates than dividends or capital gains.
- Capital gains are not taxed until they are realized — assets are actually disposed of, or upon a deemed disposition, like death, emigration or transfer.

- There are no taxable gains on the sale of a principal residence.
- Pensions are added to income in full, with the only offsetting provision being the $1,000 pension income amount which is worth, on average, $270.
- Inherited life insurance policies are tax exempt.
- Old Age Security (OAS) will be subject to a clawback when net income is around $60,000.
- Taxes can be disguised as user fees based on the level of net income generated. The size of deductibles for prescription drugs and per diem rates for nursing home care come to mind as examples. Therefore the structure of income withdrawals should take clawbacks of social benefits into account by focusing on net income.

Create Tax-Efficient Savings

When discussing savings for the future, ask your advisor about tax efficiency first. If you are producing income now, start with your RRSP contributions. A deposit will buy you immediate tax savings and tax deferred income growth — a double-digit return on your investment. This means, you'll accumulate twice as much for retirement as saving outside the plan. Ask your financial advisor to show you the calculations that prove this point.

While an RRSP will give you immediate income returns by way of tax savings, investments in capital assets including stocks, bonds, mutual funds, real estate and heirlooms will provide you with the opportunity of tax deferred appreciation. That is, the increase in value of your property held outside an RRSP is never taxed until disposition. This keeps your net income low, which often means you can qualify for more refundable and non-refundable tax credits or pay less in user fees, including some public prescription plans or per diem rates in personal care homes or child care placement.

When it comes to education savings, use everyone's productivity to make it happen. There should be no excuse for a child to miss an opportunity for education at a higher level in Canada. Not only are education standards and results excellent here, the cost of education itself is very reasonable by comparison to other countries. No matter what your socio-economic status today, it is a fact that your legacy will do better with education. So the best family investment plan you can make is to send your children to school.

The Statistics Canada Web site, for example, shows that the average net worth of Canadians rises dramatically with education (see Figure 8.1).

Figure 8.1
Financial Worth as a Factor of Education Received*

Education Level	% of Family Units	Average Net Worth	Median Net Worth
Less than high school	27%	$180,600	$79,600
High school graduates	23%	$226,000	$93,000
Non-university certificate	28%	$213,000	$106,100
University degree	15%	$349,400	$168,000
Master's certificate	5%	$496,000	$260,000
Degree in medicine, dentistry	1%	$767,000	$420,000

*Statistics Canada Web site: Catalogue no. 12-596-XIE.

Tax Query
How can I Give my Children their most Important Asset: Their Education?

If your children need an education savings plan, ask your advisor to develop scenarios that encompass several immediate savings options including:

- How the family can increase Canada Child Tax Benefit receipts for young children
- The value of the deposit of those receipts into the child's education fund
- The contributions of a Registered Education Savings Plan and its resulting earnings
- The contributions of the child's own work in saving for education
- The value of Registered Retirement Savings Plan (RRSP) contributions based on the child's earned income to produce tax free withdrawals within the RRSP Lifelong Learning Plan
- The contributions from other non-registered savings

Other Savings

Once current living needs and retirement and education savings obligations are met, you can save for personal lifestyle and career freedom. That brings us to other investments that produce non-registered savings. Refer back to Chapter 3. There you learned that not all investment income sources are taxed alike. Discuss your asset mix in your non-registered savings portfolios with your financial advisors, asking whether a re-balancing is necessary given current market conditions and in the process ensuring that you are getting the tax results you want, especially in mutual fund accounts.

Create a Family Powerhouse

Remember too that you can focus your tax-efficient investment strategies on family wealth creation. Even if your own RRSP room is fully contributed, for example, you can focus on building each family member's holdings. Ask your advisor to identify the RRSP contribution room of each person, then contribute to max out their room. These transactions are attribution free, which means that your family member will be taxed on the resulting withdrawals, not you. Ask your tax advisor to explain the difference between contributing to a spouse's RRSP and a spousal RRSP in your case. The former is based on your spouse's earned income rather than yours, while the latter requires that certain holding requirements must be met.

You can also consider shoring up life, critical illness, disability or long-term care policies for some or all family members. Speak to your tax professional about all your opportunities to split income with family members to save tax dollars in the near future. Or, discuss the transfer of money or assets within the attribution rules.

In short, discuss all investment decisions in the context of the family unit as a group which will provide you with a powerhouse of inter-generational wealth accumulation opportunity. Use the productivity of each family member to grow the roots of your financial tree, looking at all their options to save for education, retirement and current needs. Finally, add tax savvy into the investment mix to maximize all of those efforts. See Advisor Check-In 8.1 for some sample questions to get you started with your advisor.

FOCUS ON DEDUCTIONS

There are six expenditures you will want to focus on with your tax pro:
1. the RRSP deduction (as previously discussed)
2. the business investment loss, resulting from investments in small business corporations
3. carrying charges, including costs of interest expenses on investment loans
4. stock options and shares deductions
5. capital loss applications
6. the $500,000 capital gains exemption.

Discuss these deductions in relation to the activity in your investment portfolio and ask your advisor to provide "what if" scenarios relating to these provisions, if you are in the process of negotiating the acquisition or disposition of new assets and their related costs. Also, if you are starting a new business, discuss whether your business structure should be that of a proprietorship or a corporation. (See also Chapter 9.)

FOCUS ON NON-REFUNDABLE TAX CREDITS

There are no specific non-refundable tax credits that pertain to investment income. However, the use of other available credits will increase your family's tax-free zone, that is, the amount of taxable income that can be earned before being subject to tax.

When you understand your tax-free zone, you'll be able to make a decision about how much money to withdraw to meet your after-tax needs. Therefore ask your tax advisor to identify the tax-free zones your non-refundable tax credits will create every year because the numbers change annually due to indexing.

FOCUS ON REFUNDABLE TAX CREDITS

We have discussed the impact of net income on the ability to tap into federal refundable tax credits, the Canada Child Tax Benefit and the GST/HST Credit for example, and explained that the highest marginal tax rates apply, subject to clawbacks of social benefits. Net income is also used to compute provincial credits, where available, and non-refundable tax credits, discussed earlier. Your investment income strategies — especially the use of your RRSP contribution room — have a big bearing on the distribution of these social benefits, so be sure you and your tax advisor fully understand the implications of any taxable income generation on net income.

TAX PRO COACH
Your Strategic Plan to Tax Savings for Canadian Investors
Manage your investment income and capital formation strategies more proactively. Your biggest enemy is not market volatility or even tax rates, but time. Start with these questions and discover all your options with your tax advisor:

- How can I arrange my affairs to increase the amount of after-tax dollars available to me?
- Can I better utilize tax provisions available to me to generate new savings, when, in fact, I am having trouble simply covering with day-to-day living needs with my current income level?

- How can I save in a tax-efficient way for my children's education and my retirement when I need to pay the mortgage today and I'd like to take a vacation now and then?
- Can you develop "what if" scenarios to show me how tax preferred education and retirement savings can help me meet my financial planning goals?
- How much money will my children need for their education? How do I keep it safe from taxation if they decide not to attend school?
- How can I leave something behind to help my children and, in turn, their children?
- How can I build capital assets, upon which appreciation in value is deferred?
- How can I use the provisions of the tax system to leverage my income and capital to accumulate more wealth?
- What is the most tax-effective way to build an emergency fund?
- How can my family unit as a whole earn and save more tax efficiently?

Advisor Check-In 8.1
Questions About Tax-Efficient Family Investment Planning

- What investment should be made first: contributions to an RRSP or pay down the mortgage?
- Should I buy a home or pay off my credit cards first?
- When does it make sense to borrow for investment purposes?
- What is the most effective way to start an education savings plan for my kids?
- How can I best move tax-paid capital to my lower earning spouse or children?
- Can I draw up a loan and lend my spouse money for investments?
- How much should I contribute to my and my spouse's RRSP this year?
- What is the best way to split income with my minor and adult children so they can make investments?
- Can I provide my low-income parent with money for an investment so that resulting earnings are taxed to her?
- What are the tax implications of financing my spouse's business?
- How can I use the insurance requirements of my family as an investment tool?
- How can I structure my income sources in the future to minimize and defer tax?
- When should I give the shares of my small business corporation to my adult children?
- How can I use up the tax losses I have incurred in the marketplace to my best advantage?
- Can I transfer my tax losses to my spouse, who has a higher income?

Advisor Check-In 8.2
Preparing to Discuss Investments with Your Advisor

A. TAX TERMS TO EXPLORE

To communicate well with your tax advisor about your investments, here are some basic concepts to know. Discuss these further with your advisor and ask her to summarize your holdings as of today's date. Then discuss what the holdings must be to meet your income and capital formation goals.

REGISTERED INVESTMENTS
- Registered Retirement Savings Plan (RRSP)
- Lifelong Learning Plan (LLP)
- Home Buyers' Plan (HBP)
- Registered Pension Plan (RPP)
- Registered Education Savings Plan (RESP)

NON-REGISTERED INVESTMENTS
- Guaranteed Investment Certificates (GICs)
- Shares
- Mutual funds
- Bonds
- Real estate
- Residences
- Heirlooms

Now that you know the basic terminology used in investment planning, turn to Part B for some specific questions regarding the taxation of investments. Ask any follow-up questions until you fully understand your advisor's response.

B. HOW YOUR INVESTMENTS WILL BE TAXED

QUESTION	UNDERSTANDING THE RESPONSE
Should I change my asset mix to earn more or less interest?	You are required to report 100% of interest earned on your return every year even if that includes interest on compounding investments. Although the amounts are accrued, and not yet actually received, they are added to your income. This makes interest earnings less tax efficient than capital gains or dividends. Discuss this with your advisor.
Can I change the ratio of income reporting from year to year in my joint accounts?	The person who contributed the principal, earned in her own right, must report the income generated by these accounts. How have you been reporting this in the past and has your reporting been consistent? How have you tracked the information? Is it linked to interest costs of making investment loans?

QUESTION	UNDERSTANDING THE RESPONSE
Do I have options in claiming the dividends my spouse and I have earned from our investments?	Reporting dividends is tricky. You'll note two boxes on your T Slips: actual and taxable dividends. You received the actual amount which is smaller than the taxable amount. The dividend tax credit offsets this, but dividends still increase your net income, the figure that determines the tax credits. If you pay dividends from your small business corporation to minor children, ask your tax advisor about the high taxes this could cause.
What are the tax consequences of my capital gains and losses?	To have a useful discussion about your investments with your tax and financial advisors, take the time to read some definitions. Assets that are disposed of during the tax year for more or less than their *adjusted cost base* will result in a capital gain or loss. This can happen when an income-producing asset is sold for more than its cost or when there is a *deemed disposition*; that is, death, emigration or when an asset is transferred to a relative. When you discuss *capital gains* and *losses* with your tax pro you'll be asked to look for the adjusted cost base figure. That's the original cost of your asset when you acquired it, plus additions (like mutual fund distributions) or improvements (like the deck you put on the cottage last year). Finding the adjusted cost base can be really challenging. Only a portion of the capital gain you incur is added to income. This is called the *taxable gain*. Since October 18, 2000, the taxable gain is 50% of the capital gain. When the disposition of your assets results in *capital losses*, they will be deductible against other capital gains of the current year, in the three preceding years or against future gains. They are not, however, deductible against other income. Note that *losses* on *depreciable assets*, such as buildings, equipment, cars, etc., that are used to earn income are not capital losses but are deductible as terminal losses.

Note: When you lose money you have invested in a Canadian controlled small business corporation, you will be able to take a tax deduction in the current year that applies a portion of the loss against other income. If the loss is not fully absorbed, it can be carried back to offset other income of the three immediately preceding years. Balances still remaining can offset other income earned for seven years in the future and after this, unapplied losses become capital losses which can be carried forward indefinitely, but only applied against capital gains. This is called a business investment loss.

QUESTION	UNDERSTANDING THE RESPONSE
Do I have to report foreign investment earnings?	You must tell your tax advisor about any income you may be earning from foreign pensions or in foreign accounts or from foreign property of any kind. If you paid foreign taxes, your tax advisor will be preparing an offsetting foreign tax credit to help you avoid double taxation. You may also be required to file foreign tax returns, depending on jurisdiction.
How do I report my investment loan interest and other costs of making investments?	If you have taken out a loan for investment purposes, it is important to report interest paid specific to the investment income or potential investment income. This must be carefully tracked. You may not deduct interest paid on any portion of the loan made for personal purposes or for the acquisition of registered investments such as an RRSP or RESP. Remember that it is possible to make inter-family investment loans at today's low prescribed rates (3% at the time of writing) and thereby properly transfer funds from high earners to low ones. This cost must be paid by January 30 of the new year and is reported as a carrying charge by the payor and as income by the recipient. Discuss this with your tax and financial planner.

CHAPTER 9

Accumulating Wealth as An Entrepreneur

- Analyze the risk and tax benefits of entrepreneurship
- Understand how losses can be beneficial, tax-wise
- Make use of deductions to business profits
- Understand the tax consequences when you acquire new assets
- Reduce net business income for increased tax credits
- Audit-proof your tax filing affairs

Want to know how to build your wealth to a resounding crescendo? Become an entrepreneur.

According to Statistics Canada, those who are self-employed will have a median net worth that's more than two-and-a-half times greater than those who are paid employees. When you work for yourself you build both income and equity; when you work for someone else, you generally take home income only.

The income you earn as an employee is taxed away, usually every two weeks. If you build equity in your own small businesses — providing you build something that can be sold to another — you have the opportunity to accrue increased value in your equity on a completely tax deferred basis. In addition, if you build that equity within a qualifying small business corporation, you will reap the benefits of a tax-free gain, thanks to the $500,000 capital gains exemption.

So, for example, if each of the four adult members of your family owned one share of a corporation that sold for $2,000,000, that lump-sum windfall would stay all in the family — tax free. This is a great way to strengthen the family financial tree.

But, entrepreneurship also involves great risk and not everyone is up for it. Entrepreneurs must be prepared to spend first, reap rewards later. They must live in the future because that's where the next dollar is made. Their decision-making must be based on vision and foresight, rather than hindsight.

The tax system recognizes the risk entrepreneurs face in building their businesses, providing a series of tax provisions that allow for the claiming of non-capital losses against other income of the year, the three prior years and for up to seven years in the future. This is a form of income averaging that recognizes that the affairs of the business evolve on a continuum.

Yet, small business owners — even those who follow the rules — often find themselves in the middle of an expensive and time-consuming tax audit.

In fact, the onus of proof is on the taxpayer. This is when your relationship with your tax professional can really pay dividends. Even with all the documents, receipts and logs, you must show that you have been operating a viable business — not a hobby — which, perhaps despite recent losses, has a reasonable expectation of profit in the future. Fortunately, the courts have ruled again and again that taxpayers must be allowed to structure their affairs in such a way as to pay the least amount of taxes possible. In addition, income from a business is not necessary to validate the claiming of deductions or losses; it is enough that there is an expectation of income from the expenditures. Finally, there is no timeframe within which reasonable profits must occur. It differs with every business and that's where the business owner has some important controls.

In fact, it is the business owner who knows the future. This can be documented easily in formal business plans and records of networking, proposals and presentations that may turn into future business contracts. It is important, therefore, to master your data harvesting and retrieval skills and get a great advisory team behind you.

KEY TAX ISSUES FOR YOUR ADVISOR

As a small business owner you must focus on tax cost averaging with your tax pro. You must determine how the level of taxation paid over the lifetime of the business can be averaged downward. There are many ways to do so and these are the key issues to be explored:

- **Compliance:** When must GST/HST and source remittances for payroll deductions be made and when is it necessary to issue T4 Slips? What is the deadline for filing personal tax returns (June 15 or April 30)? What is the deadline for GST/HST and payroll source deductions? When must quarterly instalment tax payments be made?

- **Tax-Efficiency:** How can business deductions and asset write-offs be maximized? How is the business activity best integrated with personal tax planning? And how is business and tax planning best integrated with other asset accumulations? How can you maximize your equity when your business is sold or transferred to another generation?
- **Family Finances:** How are family members compensated with the most tax efficiency? How does the business factor into the growth of the family financial legacy? How can the opportunities to hire family members in the business be used to split income, shore up RRSP savings and diversify each member's income?

When it comes to compliance, don't fool around. Know when to make remittances to the government for payroll deductions, sales taxes and tax returns. Penalties for non-compliance are very expensive.

Next, satisfy your lenders and your owners/shareholders. Despite the fact that you are fulfilling many roles, you must first and foremost be the chair-person of the board.

To do so, ensure that your business statements outline the performance of your enterprise clearly and allow you to make business decisions. You must also be audit-proof. Your bookkeeping must be up-to-date and provide the business statements, working papers and hard copy that you, your lenders and your tax auditor need to assess whether management is keeping your business on its road to success, including:

- **The Statement of Profits and Losses:** This statement includes your actual results of business operations for the month and how this compares to your budget.
- **The Balance Sheet:** This report shows your financial position as at a particular date: once a month, once a quarter and once a year.

Ask your tax advisors to explain the results of the enterprise from a tax point of view, as your tax statements will differ from your accounting statements in most cases. Understand how the results integrate with your personal tax filing provisions and your other investment opportunities.

FOCUS ON LOSSES

Most small businesses begin as proprietorships. That is important if you want to write off start-up losses against other income of the current or prior years. For example, if in the past you've been a business executive and you have recently retired to start your own company, you could recover past income tax withholding on your executive salary by writing off excess business losses. This could be a way to fund other start-up costs and recover money. Ask your tax advisor about this possibility. If you incorporate right away, you will only be able to carry business losses forward to offset corporate profits in the next seven years because you have no corporate income or structure to carry back to.

Discuss the use of business and tax structures to achieve the results you want from the start-up costs incurred. Ask your tax advisor to prepare a "what if" scenario so that you can both judge the effectiveness of the carry-back and include the tax refunds in your cash flow projections. Your previous income structure should be reviewed over the past three years to make this determination.

FOCUS ON INCOME

Ask your tax advisor detailed questions regarding the reporting of your business income. You'll need to determine whether you are using a cash or accrual method of accounting. Barter transactions will have to be recorded. Returns, allowances and discounts will affect income reporting and you'll need to account for inventory purchases. Recording personal use of business expenditures and assets is important to track. You may also want to instruct your bookkeeper to break out various income categories for information purposes. You also may have options in selecting your fiscal year end. Your advisor will be able to discuss the pros and cons of all these considerations with you. You can also refer to Advisor Check-In 9.1 for some sample questions to get you started.

FOCUS ON DEDUCTIONS

To make judgment calls about the deductibility of your business expenses, you need to make sure that they are reasonable under the circumstances, tied to income-producing activities and not for personal living expenses. Those are the three cardinal rules. Provided you keep these rules in mind, there are a number of areas where deductions can be claimed, thus reducing your taxable income. Refer to Advisor Check-In 9.1 for sample questions to put to your advisor regarding the deductibility of business expenses.

You need to break your expenditures into two categories:

1. **Operational Expenses:** These are usually 100% deductible, but there are exceptions, like the deductibility of meals and entertainment expenses, which are subject to a 50% restriction.

2. **Capital Expenditures:** These are assets with a useful life of more than one year. Their costs are subject to depreciation on your accounting statements and capital cost allowance on your tax statements. Ask your tax advisor to explain the difference.

Buy vs. Lease Option

It is very important that you understand the tax implications of your purchases. Timing is important. You will want to shore up your operational expenses before year-end to receive the tax benefits of your expenditures sooner rather than later. So remember to put gas in the car or buy office supplies you'll need soon before, rather than after, your fiscal year end.

You will also want to receive advice about whether to buy or lease the assets you use in your business. Ask your advisor to create a "what if" scenario comparing the after-tax costs of buying versus leasing. Be sure he runs the example out over a five year period.

You should know that the leasing costs are 100% deductible as an operational expense. This could increase a business loss, which may be desirable if you are wishing to maximize tax recovery from a loss carry-back. However, you'll have to have the cash flow to make the payments. The capital cost allowance mechanism, on the other hand, allows you to save the tax deduction for capital cost allowance until a future time when income may be higher and tax reductions are more beneficial. It is always taken at the taxpayer's option. Also, remember that in the year an asset is acquired, it is subject to a half year rule which means that only one-half the normal capital cost allowance claim is allowed. Therefore it is important to understand whether an asset should be acquired at the end of one tax year or at the start of another. Ask for numerical proof to help you make that decision.

Hiring Family

You'll also want to discuss the hiring of family members. There are very specific rules to follow to ensure your affairs are audit-proof. Your family members must perform work that you would otherwise need to hire someone else to do and the amount you pay must be reasonable under the circumstances. You'll need to know what source deductions to make for them and how to complete their T4 Slips. Ask your advisor how you can influence family wealth by ensuring your family employees make RRSP contributions and have coverage under group health insurance plans. You may wish to discuss how you can provide tax-free or taxable perks to them. Find out whether your relatives will be allowed to collect Employment Insurance if they leave your firm and, if not, whether premiums are necessary.

Home Office and Car Use

Partial use must be carefully tracked when you have a home office and/or a car you use for both personal and business driving. Any expenditures that have a personal use component are audit triggers and it is important that you keep documentation to justify both personal and business usage. Also know that business losses cannot be increased or created with the home office claim. You may carry forward unused deductions and apply them to business income in the future. Have your advisor keep track of this in your permanent file to be reviewed next tax season.

CPP Premiums of the Proprietor

Remember too that you will be making your own Canada Pension Plan (CPP) remittances if you are self-employed. Net income level determines the CPP premium and once you have net income in excess of $39,000 you reach the maximum contribution level. Many proprietors are caught off guard by the CPP premium — which can exceed $3,000 at its maximum, payable when the personal return is filed. This tax is extremely expensive, rising and can erode the benefits of income-splitting with family members.

RRSP and Child Care Expenses

Other deductions on the tax return will be affected by your business results. For example, if you have a business loss and are the lower income earner in the family with little other income, you will be the one who must claim the child care expenses. If your income is very low, you may also wish to discuss whether all of your RRSP contribution should be deducted this year. It's possible to carry forward undeducted contributions for use in the future when income is higher.

FOCUS ON NON-REFUNDABLE TAX CREDITS

The proprietor and his tax pro must keep the available non-refundable tax credits in mind when determining the use of optional provisions available to reduce the net income of the business. For example, if your available tax-free zone is around $8,000 with your basic personal amount and some medical expenses, reducing net income down to $8,000 with optional capital cost allowance deductions is just the thing to do. Ask your tax pro about the possibility of saving the balance of your write-offs to reduce future income.

When your net business income is very low, your spouse may be able to claim you as a dependant. Your advisor may also make reference to the fact that other non-refundable tax credits will be affected by your low income.

For example, some of your tax credits may be transferred or claimed by your spouse for a better net effect for the whole family unit. Everyone in the family should be sure to collect receipts for medical costs, the charity donations and the political contributions. Your advisor will decide who should claim these for your best benefit. Be sure you receive sufficient information about your net business income early enough to make proper decisions regarding tax-efficient investments like RRSP and Labour-Sponsored Investment Funds purchases for the whole family. Again, ask your advisor to prepare some "what if" scenarios to help you understand your tax savings opportunities better.

FOCUS ON REFUNDABLE TAX CREDITS

When net income of the family is reduced by business losses, it is possible that refundable tax credits like the Canada Child Tax Benefit (CCTB) or the GST/HST Credit will be created or increased. Your tax pro will tell you what to expect. Your role is to take any of these windfall amounts and invest them properly.

FOCUS ON INVESTMENTS

You'll have a number of questions for your tax advisor surrounding your investment in your business enterprise or the investment of your business profits elsewhere. First and foremost, position yourself to maximize your family members' and your RRSP savings. Next, enquire about whether your business structure enables your family to maximize the $500,000 capital gains exemption, should the business be sold to a third party in the future. That will build a substantial future for you and your family. Or you may want to keep the business in the family so you'll need to determine the best time to pass the assets of the business or corporation on to your children or spouse. Ask your advisor about an estate freeze and how you can use it to your advantage. If you currently run a proprietorship, find out the benefits and pitfalls of incorporation.

Discuss your personal compensation structure with a view to minimizing taxes: find out whether you should take a salary, dividends or bonus from your small business corporation and if you can pay dividends to your spouse and minor children. Determine the tax consequences of these options with your advisor. Proprietors must report net income or losses from the business on their personal returns. In some cases, it may be advantageous to discuss a partnership.

When it comes to acquiring assets, you'll want to know whether it's wisest to lease, borrow or buy. You'll also want to ask if all the interest you pay to lenders is deductible and whether interest on capital asset acquisitions should be claimed as a deduction or as part of the asset cost.

Finally, be sure to invest any benefits from the tax system wisely to ensure that you don't have all your eggs in one basket. You need a well-diversified portfolio outside of your business affairs to protect your personal wealth.

TAX PRO COACH
Your Strategic Plan to Maximize the Tax Benefits of Business Ownership

Manage your business affairs with a clear understanding of the tax consequences of your decision-making all year long. Review these ideas with your advisor:

- How can I maximize tax benefits on start-up losses?
- How can I build RRSP contribution room running a business? Can my RRSP deductions help increase losses to reduce taxes in the current year or to offset taxes paid in prior years?
- When is it to my tax advantage to acquire or dispose of capital assets?
- How can I best involve my family members in the business? Can I help my spouse finance business acquisitions on an attribution free basis? Can I borrow from my spouse and deduct interest costs? Is it to my advantage to hire my family members in my business?
- How can I help my employees reduce the taxes they pay by offering tax-advantaged remuneration packages?
- How do the tax filing results of my small business integrate with my personal income tax return? How will the social benefits we qualify for be affected?
- How can I deduct the costs of my company car and my home office?
- How can I diversify family income with incorporation?
- How can I pay the least amount of taxes on the sale of business equity?
- What are the tax consequences if I lose my business equity or have to declare bankruptcy?
- What are my GST/HST obligations?
- What do I need to know about audit-proofing my returns?

Advisor Check-In 9.1
Questions About My Business — Income, Expenses and Assets

ABOUT MY INCOME

- At what income level does it make more sense to earn my business income inside a corporation rather than a proprietorship?
- In order to grow my new business, I need capital. Is there any way to get help from the tax department to get that capital?
- Why is it that the business statements my bookkeeper prepares don't have the same figures as the business statement I file with my tax return?
- Cash is short so sometimes I trade my services for supplies or services I need. How am I supposed to report that? No one is making any money here so do I really need to report it at all?
- I'm negotiating a multi-year contract. How will the timing of the payments affect my taxes?
- My wife has been working for me as an employee in my business. Things are going well now so I want to make her a partner. How do I report income in that case?
- One of my clients didn't pay his bill last year and it's still outstanding. Do I have to pay taxes on that income if I don't have it?
- When do I have to collect and remit GST/HST on my income?
- How do I make my income reporting audit-proof?
- What impact does my inventory level have on my income and how should this be managed to provide me with the best tax and business advantages?

ABOUT MY BUSINESS EXPENSES

- Is it more advantageous to buy or lease a car for business purposes?
- What expenses are not deductible from my business income?
- What expenses are partially deductible?
- How can I tell if an expenditure is reasonable for tax purposes?
- How can I justify the existence of my business enterprise if no money has come in yet?
- How will my business losses be written off?
- How do I claim home office expenses?
- Can I claim the costs of hiring my spouse or child in my business?
- Is there an advantage to hiring sub-contractors rather than employees in my business?
- How often do I have to remit employment source deductions?
- I heard that if I put the name of my business on the side of my car for advertising purposes then I'm using my car for business all the time. Is that true?
- Every year at inventory time I find things are missing. How do I write off those items?
- My husband and son work in my business. What employee benefits can I provide them without increasing their taxes or affecting my deductions for these costs?

- My wife has another job and I need some help in my business. Does it make more sense for me to hire a stranger or have my wife quit her other job and come to work for me?
- My husband wants to work for me in my business, but we have two small kids at home. If he works from home, can we write off part of our home expenses? Can we deduct child care costs?
- When items sold in our business are returned, they are often not in resalable condition so I take· them home and use them rather than throw them out. Will that cause me any grief with the tax department?
- Our family will eat meals we cook at our restaurant. How is this accounted for?
- Can the new roof on our building be written off in full?
- What is the income level at which I pay the maximum Canada Pension Plan premiums on my business income?
- How many conferences and seminars can I attend during the year and can I deduct travel expenses for my family if they accompany me?
- Are my club memberships and dining room charges deductible if I entertain clients there?
- Can my company make my Registered Retirement Savings Plan contributions for me? What are the tax implications?
- How do I capitalize on the equity I am building in my business? What are the tax consequences on the sale of my business?
- Is it better to make a charitable contribution through my business or make it personally?
- I got a parking ticket while at a client's office last month. Can I write off the fine?
- How much better off would we be as a family if I gave my daughter a summer job to pay her college tuition instead of just paying it myself?

ABOUT MY ASSET ACQUISITIONS AND DISPOSITIONS

- How do I claim a deduction for money spent on the acquisition of capital assets?
- How do I account for improvements I'd like to make to my assets?
- Is it a good idea to depreciate my assets over time?
- What happens if I forgot to list an asset on my return a couple of years ago?
- I'm going to have to expand my business premises soon, but real estate prices have gone up since I bought the current building. How much tax will I have to pay when I sell the old building and how will that affect my down payment on the new one?
- I'm going to need to replace some equipment soon. For tax purposes is it better to buy the new equipment sooner or later?
- I want to open a new location in another part of town. Is it better to rent the space or buy the building?
- I have an offer to buy my business but the buyer wants to pay by instalments over several years. How does this affect my taxes?
- What are the tax consequences if I retire and let my son take over my business? Would it be better if I just hired him to manage the business?

CHAPTER 10

Executors — What You Need to Know

- Understand your role and responsibilities to CCRA as executor
- Keep the future of the beneficiaries in mind
- Investigate the deceased's past finances and prior-filed returns to uncover tax savings
- Use this experience to enhance your own estate planning

Demographically, Canada is experiencing the greying of its largest tax-paying constituency — the baby boomers. Currently giving care to their aged parents, this powerful tax base is preparing for its own late life cycle in the midst of shocking economic turbulence. While the boomers contemplate whether they can afford the type of retirement they may have dreamed of, many are also in the position of executor for their parents' estates and inheritors of significant wealth. It is important to work with tax advisors inter-generationally so that you can know the essence of the directives in the will and the important task of asset valuation now. Empowered with this knowledge, important estate preservation decisions can be made during life. For example, it may make more sense — tax-wise — to give or transfer assets during life, rather than at death. These decisions, including the choices left in filing the final tax returns can leave — or diminish — a substantial legacy.

KEY TAX ISSUES FOR YOUR ADVISOR

There are five key issues to explore with tax pros regarding the tax consequences of death:

1. What tax return(s) must be filed for the deceased? What are the options in managing taxes payable upon the deemed disposition of assets at death?
2. What options are available in reporting income sources on the final return and after death?
3. How can Registered Retirement Savings Plan (RRSP) contribution room be maximized in the year of death?
4. How can non-refundable tax credits be maximized on the final return and by survivors?
5. What refundable tax credits should be claimed at death and on which return?

WHAT CCRA REQUIRES

When a taxpayer dies, at least one final, mandatory tax return must be submitted by the executor. Several elective or optional returns may also be filed, depending on the income sources of the deceased. The date of death and the choices made in reporting income and capital dispositions on the final or optional returns can significantly reduce taxes owing at death. They will also have a bearing on future tax returns of the spouse and beneficiaries. Discuss these options and deadlines with your tax advisor.

The executor may also wish to take advantage of important tax savings opportunities on current year returns using special provisions for refundable and non-refundable tax credits. It is not unusual, therefore, for several tax filing scenarios to be attempted before the best benefit can be found for the estate and beneficiaries.

Deadlines and Options

A final, mandatory return must be filed within certain guidelines, but there are elective returns which may be filed for greater tax savings.

Final, Mandatory Return

The final, mandatory return covers the period from January 1 to the date of death in the year of death. If death occurs in the first ten months of the year, the return must be filed no later than April 30 of the year immediately following the year of death. If death occurs in the last two months of the year, the return must be filed six months after the date of death.

However, if there is income from a business to be included on the final return or the return of the deceased's spouse or common-law partner, the final, mandatory return must be filed no later than June 15 of the year immediately following the year of death if the date of death occurs in the first ten months of the year. If death occurs in the last two months of the year, the deadline for filing is six months after the date of death.

Elective Returns

There are three possible types of returns that can be filed to cover different types of income and provide tax savings: rights or things, income from a partnership or proprietorship or income from a testamentary trust. Discuss the benefits of dividing up and reporting these income sources on separate returns with your advisor, who may wish to prepare several "what if" scenarios to determine the best combination of results. The primary advantage is the ability to use the personal amounts on each return, thereby reducing overall taxes payable. The deadlines for filing these returns varies from six months to one year after the date of death to June 15 of the year following death. Discuss these deadlines with your advisor and be sure to harvest and deliver all the appropriate data required.

KEY PLANNING OBJECTIVES FOR THE FINAL RETURN

Unusually high taxes can be triggered on the final tax returns because of the deemed disposition rules. That is, assets owned by the deceased are deemed disposed of at the date of death, usually at their fair market value. However, those assets may be rolled over to a surviving spouse or common-law partner or, in some cases, to children at their adjusted cost base. Deposits within RRSPs or Registered Retirement Investment Funds (RRIFs) must also be rolled over to a spouse or children or taxed at death. There are some ways to avoid taxes due to deemed disposition, discussed below under Focus on Investments.

Income earned by the deceased, on the other hand, is reported on a pro-rata basis from January 1 to the date of death. Income earned after death is taxed either to the estate or in the hands of the surviving spouse or beneficiaries. What this means is that bereaved families must attend not only to the final tax filing affairs of the deceased, but also understand that the survivors' income could fluctuate dramatically in the year of death and beyond. Tax preparation, therefore, must encompass several returns and several years.

In the year of death, there are also special rules for the claiming of certain deductions, losses, medical expenses, charitable donations, death benefits received through employment and the paying of tax liabilities.

The Goals of the Tax Filer

Because of these numerous options available to file the final returns of the deceased, it is important to understand the primary objectives of tax filing:

- Split income sources earned by the deceased before death onto a variety of tax returns to lower the overall tax brackets into which final income will fall. Of course, as executor you have the right to enquire about these options and to understand their benefits.
- Take full advantage of the special tax provisions available on the final and optional returns filed for the deceased, by leveraging claims allowed for certain non-refundable tax credits and enhanced claims allowed for others.
- Present the value of assets on the final return to take advantage of opportunities to select values that minimize taxes at death but also the future tax liabilities of beneficiaries who inherit the assets.
- Minimize the taxes of survivors in the current tax year and in the future.

It is also important to fully discharge the obligations of the executor, who takes on the tax filing responsibilities of the deceased.

Obligations of Executor

The executor is responsible for filing the final tax returns and making all tax payments before the proceeds of the estate are distributed to beneficiaries. She must also ensure that the clearance certificate, which CCRA issues when the final affairs of the deceased have been assessed, is received.

Should the executor fail to obtain a clearance certificate, taxes payable on subsequent assessments or reassessments by CCRA are the personal responsibility of the executor, if the assets of the estate have been distributed. Therefore, executors will generally want to work closely with the tax advisor in completing those returns on time, paying the appropriate taxes, as required, and applying for the clearance certificate.

As the executor of an estate, be sure to go one step further: ask questions of the tax advisor to assure yourself that the tax affairs and investment opportunities of the survivors are set up to their best benefit, as well as that of the deceased. While your obligations stop at the final returns, it would be responsible of you to ensure that the resources left behind are carefully positioned for future tax savings. Make sure that the bereaved are not pressured into decisions that can erode the estate significantly.

Special Rules for Paying Taxes Owing

When taxes result on the final return, it is the responsibility of the executor to pay those taxes out of the estate before distributing any of the assets.

However, if the taxes result due to the value of the deemed disposition of assets, hardship can be avoided. It is possible to make an election under subsection 159(5) to pay taxes owing in instalments over a ten-year period. This election applies to certain liabilities including income resulting from the recapture of capital cost allowance on depreciable properties, capital gains (net of losses) and rights or things filed on an optional return.

Security for payment must be provided if the election to pay by instalment is made and the first payment must be made at the time the final return is filed. The remaining payments must be made on or before the anniversary date. Ask your advisor about this option and she will file the correct form (Form T2075). You can expect that interest will be charged at the prescribed rate on the taxes deferred. This provision will help the executor avoid the hasty sale of assets to pay tax liabilities on deemed disposition at death, however, and enable the actual sale when market conditions are more advantageous. In addition, at that time, the actual cash will be available to pay the taxes.

FOCUS ON INCOME

Documentation requirements will vary for the purposes of filing the final returns of the deceased. Prepare a summary of all income sources received by the deceased immediately prior to death for the period January 1 to the date of death. You'll need to go to the financial institutions where the deceased had invested money and receive statements that show pro-rated interest earnings on bank accounts, guaranteed income certificates or other debt obligations held by the deceased, for the period January 1 to the date of death. Your tax or financial planner or lawyer may obtain this information for you.

In general, income received before death is reported on the final return(s) of the deceased. Income received thereafter is reported on the return the trust will file, if the income and/or assets have not been distributed, or on the return of the beneficiaries, if they have.

Perhaps the most time-consuming task of reporting income will be the obtaining of fair market valuations of all assets held by the deceased at death, as discussed later under Deemed Dispositions. See Advisor Check-In 10.1 for a summary of questions to ask and Focus on Investments later in this chapter.

Encourage Estate Planning at Tax Time

Gift-giving during a taxpayer's lifetime may result in better alternatives than leaving all inheritances to the end of life. See Chapter 5 for some insight on this subject and discuss it with your tax advisor as part of your annual estate planning review. Tax filing time is the perfect time to review your will, the value of your assets and their unrealized gains or losses. If your tax advisor does not make that part of the annual routine, be sure to bring it up this year. It's an efficient way to approach a less-than-pleasant subject.

FOCUS ON DEDUCTIONS
There are three key deductions to focus on:
1. the RRSP contribution
2. the carrying charges, if the deceased was deducting interest paid on an investment loan
3. the claim for a capital gains deduction if the deceased had shares in a qualifying small business corporation or family farm enterprise.

RRSP Concerns
A final RRSP contribution can be made, to reduce income on the deceased's final return, if the deposit is made during the tax year or within 60 days of year end and if the deceased had the required RRSP contribution room. It should be made to a spousal RRSP. Ask your tax advisor to explain the rules surrounding the transfer of RRSP and RRIF deposits to surviving members of the family. In general, a tax-free spousal rollover is available which means that the accumulations in the accounts are subsequently taxed in that surviving spouse's hands, when she withdraws the funds. Anything that is left over at death of that second surviving spouse is taxed within the survivor's final return, unless a transfer is possible to surviving minor children.

Carrying Charges
Obtain a statement of pro-rated interest costs on investment loans for the same period: January 1 to the date of death.

Capital Gains Deductions
Certain capital gains on assets may qualify for the capital gains deduction, including gains generated on deemed disposition of the shares of qualifying small business corporations or qualifying farm properties. It is important to understand the details of the qualifying criteria. Discuss these with your advisor. Ask questions about how long the shares must have been owned by the deceased before disposition, how the property must be used (actively or passively) and how the fair market value of the assets will be assessed.

There are special rules for the inheritances of family farm properties relating to both federal and provincial tax provisions. Ask your advisor to explain these to you. It is important to ensure that the values on the transfer meet twin objectives: minimization of taxes on death of the owner and later on disposition by the heirs. There are some options your advisor can work with to accomplish these goals, as described below.

FOCUS ON INVESTMENTS

As outlined earlier in this chapter, income earned on invested assets — interest, dividends, rents or royalties — is generally pro-rated for the period January 1 to the date of death and then reported on the final return of the deceased. In the case of the transfer of assets to a trust or family members, special rules apply in assessing the tax liability at death.

Deemed Dispositions at Death Require Valuation

The death of a taxpayer triggers a deemed disposition of assets, which in general are rolled over to the surviving spouse at their adjusted cost base resulting in a tax-free transfer of assets. It is possible, however, to elect to use fair market value on some or all of the assets on transfer. This could be of tax benefit if your tax advisor can arrange to use up capital loss balances the deceased may have had and, in the process, raise the cost base of the transferred assets so that the surviving spouse will have to pay less tax on capital appreciation of the transferred assets in the future. Ask about this option.

For assets which are bequeathed to others, the proceeds of disposition are generally the fair market value of the assets at death. The one exception is the transfer of qualified farm property to a child (or parent) which may be made at any value between the taxpayer's cost and the fair market value. For sample questions regarding tax definitions and facts, ask your tax advisor to review the definitions of the classifications of the assets presented in Advisor Check-in 10.2 and to explain how the valuations you seek will impact the returns of the deceased and your family members. You'll need to understand how to seek information regarding the assets' adjusted cost base (original cost or value plus the cost of any improvements to the asset while the deceased owned it), as well as its fair market value just before death. This can be a big job. Find out what documentation is needed to pass the final audit.

If you find the value of assets has diminished over time, the resulting capital losses may be claimed against income from other sources in the year of death and, if they exceed income in the year of death, they may be applied against income in the prior year, which will result in an income tax refund. Ask your tax advisor about this lucrative option and provide information about the deceased's prior-filed returns at least three years back. Look for evidence of missed capital loss reporting. If you find it, your advisor may be able to adjust the deceased's prior-filed returns to enable you to maximize loss claims on the final return.

Prior Capital Gains Elections

Further tax savings are possible if the deceased previously made a capital gains election to pre-report accrued gains held on February 22, 1994. This provision allowed taxpayers to use up their $100,000 capital gains deduction, which was eliminated as of that date. Look for Form T664 from 1994 and keep it with the will to ensure that legal representatives do not overlook this important election when filing the final return.

FOCUS ON FAMILY

The following are the key issues to discuss with your tax pro when a family member dies:

- How do beneficiaries report the receipt of lump sums and income amounts after their loved one's death?
- What personal amounts should be claimed and by whom in the year of death?

Changes for Families

Everyone's tax filing profile changes when a family member dies. In fact, income levels generally don't settle down to a normal range for a couple of years. It is therefore most important to work closely with your tax advisor to ensure you are making the best tax planning choices for the year of death and the following year.

The most important change in the case of spouses is that investment income sources will now be reported on one person's return which can cause that income to be taxed at a higher marginal rate. In addition, income can be reduced because Old Age Security is lost for the deceased spouse. Finally, quarterly instalment tax payments may be initiated, increased or decreased as a result of the special circumstances. Talk over all these eventualities with your tax advisor.

Lump Sums and Income Receipts of Survivors

Many sources of income and capital are often received when someone in the family dies (see Figure 10.1). Ask your advisors to help you manage re-investments by carefully discussing your investment objectives in the short term (one year) and the longer term (two to five years). It is often best to simply invest in a guaranteed investment in the short term, until decision-making becomes clearer based on the composition of the new family unit.

Figure 10.1
Sources of Income and Capital to Beneficiaries

Taxable	Not Taxable
Canada Pension Plan lump sum death benefit	Life insurance policy proceeds
Employment Income, pension income, interest income: after date of death are taxed to recipient	Unused sick benefits paid as a lump sum death benefit by employer: up to $10,000 received is tax exempt
Accrued gains on assets transferred to the beneficiaries after death	Debts extinguished by bequest (normal debt forgiveness rules do not apply)
Registered Retirement Savings Plan/ Registered Retirement Income Plan benefits received after death	Amounts rolled over into beneficiaries' RRSPs or annuities; Lifelong Learning Plan or Home Buyers' Plan repayment schedules taken over by beneficiaries

Life Insurance Policy Proceeds

Proceeds from a life insurance policy form an important part of an estate. The benefits are received tax free and can make a substantial difference to your survivors. The problem is that during a taxpayer's lifetime, they are financed by after-tax premiums which many cannot afford. Speak to your tax advisor about using specific tax provisions — like the tax credits generated when an investment is made into a Labour-Sponsored Investment Fund — to fund insurance premiums.

Non-Refundable Tax Credits

One of the reasons to choose to file several optional returns for the deceased is that full personal credits are receivable on each return, thereby reducing taxes more substantially than in normal filing years. However, it is also important for your tax advisor to do both spouses' returns several times to ensure that personal tax credit transfer options are also maximized. This is often the subject of several "what if" scenarios, especially if there are lots of losses to report or lots of medical and charitable receipts.

Personal Tax Credits
If the deceased, who may normally have been the higher income earner, passes away early in the year, the net income up to the date of death will be very low. This may allow the surviving spouse to claim the amount for spouse or common-law partner or transfer the age amount, pension income amount, disability amount or tuition/education amounts to that survivor's return.

But have your advisor use caution. Many who care for a terminally ill patient fail to make claims for the caregiver amount, the disability amount and medical expenses, all of which can be claimed by adjusting prior-filed returns. However, if they can be claimed immediately, the benefits can help with expensive drug costs or non-deductible funeral expenses. Speak to your tax advisors about this if you are the advocate for the patient or the caregiver.

Medical Expenses
As well, other special provisions allow the claiming of medical expenses in the best 24-month period including the date of death (normally this is the best 12-month period ending in a tax year).

Charitable Donations
Amounts up to 100% of the deceased's net income on the final return can be claimed. Charitable donations that exceed that ceiling can be carried back one year to reduce income, again using the 100% of net income ceiling. This is normally 75% on other returns. Also, any unclaimed amounts given in the five years before death can be claimed on the final return. So, again it will pay to do some digging for these documents to empower your tax pro.

TAX PRO COACH
Your Strategic Plan to Tax Savings in the Year of Death
Analyze and manage tax filing options for each member of the family when there is a death to ensure the deceased's ultimate financial lifetime achievements. Review these questions with the tax pro, in advance if possible:

- How should an executor be chosen and what tax filing obligations will this person have?
- What financial and prior tax documents do I need to locate in order to file the final return?
- Should I meet with the lawyer and tax advisor separately or together? Where do their responsibilities overlap?
- How should I handle prior errors and omissions on tax returns filed by the deceased after death?
- How can I best assist the family? Which tax credits are transferable and who should receive the refundable tax credits?

Advisor Check-In 10.1
Questions to Ask Advisors

ABOUT INCOME REPORTING FOR THE DECEASED AND BENEFICIARIES

- What returns must be filed for a deceased person and what are the filing deadlines?
- What income sources are reported by survivors?
- How is business income reported when the business survives its owner?
- Must declared but unpaid dividends be reported on the final return?
- By whom is a declared but unpaid employment bonus reported?
- Must matured but not yet cashed bond coupons be reported?
- Which income sources are reported on the final and elective returns and which are reported by survivors?

ABOUT DEDUCTIONS AND CREDITS

- What documentation is necessary and how should it be ordered?
- What tax deductions and tax credits do family members qualify for when there is a death?

Advisor Check-In 10.2
Tax Facts About Asset Dispositions

Ask your tax advisor to review the definitions of the classifications of assets below and how the valuations you seek will impact the returns of the deceased and her family members.

ASSET CLASSIFICATION	DOCUMENTATION NEEDED
Qualified small business corporation shares	• Slips: T5, T3 for interest or dividends declared • Interest costs: obtain statement from financial institution • Valuation details; articles of incorporation • Income and expense statements, balance sheets • Details of estate freezes; transfers to family members
Qualified farm property	• Corporation: as above • Proprietorship: details of farm income and expenses; balance sheet valuation on land, inventory, assets, purchase and sale of assets
Mutual funds and publicly traded shares (note: stock splits do not result in tax consequence until disposition)	• Slips: T5 or T3 • Details adjusted cost base and brokerage fees — obtain statement from financial institutions
Real estate rentals	• Statement of income and expenses • Asset valuations, purchase and sale documents • Cost of improvements, appraisals
Depreciable property	• Asset acquisitions, dispositions and fair market value at time of death
Debt obligations like bonds, promissory notes	• Slips: T5 or T3 • Self-reported private holdings
Mortgage foreclosures and repossessions	• Provide documentation
Personal use property	• Asset descriptions and valuations of personal residences and other significant personal use property • Documents to support sale or transfer values
Listed personal property	• Asset descriptions and valuations of family heirlooms, stamp and coin collections, art, jewels, etc. • Documents to support sale or transfer values

CHAPTER 11

At A Glance

You now understand the tax basics and how to use tax filing profiles when you work with your advisor. This chapter looks at 30 of the most commonly overlooked tax savings opportunities — at a glance — to present you with what you need to know, what documents you need to bring and what questions you need to ask when you make your annual tax filing visit to your advisor.

There is no question that being prepared for your visit with your tax advisor can save time and money on your tax preparation fees and enable you to meet your ultimate goal of keeping more of your hard earned dollars in your pocket through tax savings. We hope you will find this chapter especially useful in isolating, with your advisors, every tax benefit you are entitled to. Skim through it not just once, but before every visit to your advisor or whenever there is a significant change in your personal or financial affairs.

What's Changed in this Tax Filing Year?

Month	What's Changed/Happened?
Jan	Jan went back to school part-time; child care expenses paid
Feb	Jan inheritance; topped up RRSPs for Jan and Bob
Mar	Bob took a loan to buy shares in the market, paid interest
Apr	Bob started new job: commission sales with requirement to use car
May	Braces for daughter Kelly
Jun	Bob: new group health plan: premiums paid through source deductions
Jul	Child tax benefit cheques arrive: open separate account for kids
Aug	Bob: purchased computer for home office and a cell phone
Sep	Bob: took a 20% gain on shares; bought family cottage
Oct	Jan arranges to buy Canada Savings Bonds on payroll deduction plan
Nov	Bob sold mutual funds at a loss to offset his gains
Dec	Donated to charity. Bob's severely disabled mother comes to live with the family. Kelly bought new glasses.

To begin make a list of personal events that were new in your (and your family's) life in the past tax year similar to the one in the chart above. Then, make a list of the questions you have regarding each event.

These At A Glance features will help you with 30 of the most common subjects Canadian taxpayers ask of their tax advisors. If you have others, you may wish to use a similar format to investigate your tax savings opportunities and empower your advisors with the information they need to help you arrange your affairs within the framework of the law to pay the least taxes possible over the long run.

At a Glance Features

#1 INCOME THAT'S NOT TAXED

What You Need to Know
As a Canadian resident, you are taxable on your world income. However, the following types of Canadian source income are exempt from tax in Canada.

- GST/HST Credit and Canada Child Tax Benefit (CCTB)
- Lottery winnings
- Inheritances
- Life insurance policy proceeds
- Income earned on a reserve by a status Indian
- Income of an official of NATO or any of its subsidiaries
- Most amounts received because of disability or death as a result of war service
- Pension payments, allowances and other compensation received because of an injury, disability or death as a result of serving as a member in the RCMP
- Workers' compensation,* social assistance* and net federal supplements*

These income types (*) must be included in your net income for the purposes of calculating your refundable and non-refundable credits.

Any income earned from investing exempt income is taxable. Therefore you will want the lowest earner in the family to earn that investment income, if possible.

Documents or Information Needed
- Records of how the receipts listed above were invested and by whom
- Source documents (T Slips, etc.) for the income marked by the asterisk (*)
- Any other paperwork to justify the receipt of this income

Questions for Your Advisor
- Who should apply for the GST/HST and CCTB credits?
- Whose name should lottery tickets be bought in?
- How should the funds from an inheritance be used to maximize tax savings?
- How should life insurance policy proceeds be invested to minimize tax on income?

#2 CLAIMING CARRY-FORWARD AMOUNTS FROM PREVIOUS YEARS

What You Need to Know

Many tax provisions will affect more than one taxation year. When you start working with a new advisor, it is important that you tell her of any carry-forward amounts from prior years that are relevant to your current and future tax situations. Some of the important items are listed below, together with the relevant years for which information is required:

Losses of Other Years
- Business investment losses (1995 to present)
- Farming or fishing losses (1993 to present)
- Restricted farm losses (1993 to present)
- Other non-capital losses (1995 to present)
- Limited personal property losses (1995 to present)
- Other capital losses (1972 to present)

Other Amounts
- Student loan interest (1998 to present)
- Minimum tax carry-over (1995 to present)
- Unused charitable donations (1997 to present)

Still other amounts may be claimed anytime but require a receipt including moving expenses, tuition and education amounts and unclaimed RRSP (and spousal RRSP) contributions.

Documents or Information Needed
- Copies of prior years' returns are the best source of carry-forward information
- Copy of Form T664 from 1994 to show any elections made on capital property

Questions for Your Advisor
- How far back must I search to provide you with the information you require?
- Will copies of my tax returns provide enough information?

#3 PAYING YOUR TAXES BY INSTALMENT

What You Need to Know

If you owe at least $2,000 when you file your tax return this year (and in at least one of the previous two years), you will be required to make instalment payments for next year's taxes. CCRA will send you an instalment notice.

However, if your circumstances change, you can also change the amount of your instalment payments. For example, if your income will be significantly less than last year's, you can reduce your instalment payment schedule.

Documents or Information Needed

- Tax returns from the previous three years
- Estimate of this year's income, deductions and credits

Questions for Your Advisor

- Am I in a position to reduce the tax instalments I am paying?
- What information is needed to help you apply for this reduction?

#4 SPLITTING INCOME WITH YOUR SPOUSE

What You Need to Know

A spousal amount of up to approximately $6,500 can be claimed if you are supporting your spouse; however it is eroded when your spouse makes more than about $650. If you put money or assets into your spouse's hands, you could be subject to the attribution rules on the investment earnings. The following, however, are legitimate ways to have family income taxed in the hands of your spouse:

- Have your spouse save any income earned in her own right. The income earned by investing this money is your spouse's income.
- Draw up a loan agreement with your spouse to lend her money to invest. As long as the loan rate is at the prescribed rate (or higher) and the interest is actually paid, the income earned on that investment will be your spouse's income. The interest on the loan is taxable to you and deductible by your spouse.
- If you have a small business, employ your spouse in the business. If the income is reasonable for the work performed, the income will be taxable to her and deductible by you.
- Set up a spousal RRSP.
- Give your spouse money to set up a small business.

Documents or Information Needed

- All income, investment and other information about spouse's personal earnings or expenditures, especially if there is no income
- Previous tax returns (to claim refundable tax credits)

Questions for Your Advisor

- How does the equity my spouse contributed to our original home impact subsequent investment earnings?
- How can I transfer my share of my real estate assets to my spouse so that she reports a portion of the income and shares in the capital gains/losses?
- Should I be claiming dividends earned by my spouse, who can't use the dividend tax credit because of her low income?
- What is the most tax-efficient way for my spouse and I to withdraw our private pension and investment accumulations?
- How should rollovers of property be structured upon the demise of the first and second spouse?
- Who should claim the refundable tax credits in the family?

#5 SPLITTING INCOME WITH YOUR CHILDREN

What You Need to Know

Because of our progressive tax system and the fact that each individual has a tax-free zone, splitting income with family members often results in a reduction of taxes.

Attribution rules have been set to ensure that you cannot simply put funds in your child's name and have the income reported by the child on a tax-free or tax-reduced basis. The following are some legitimate ways to have family income taxed in the hands of minor children:

- Deposit the Canada Child Tax Benefit (CCTB) received each month in a separate account for the child. Income earned on that account will be considered to be the child's income.
- Give the child assets that will produce capital gains (such as shares that do not pay dividends). Interest or dividends earned on assets you give to your child will be considered to be your income, but capital gains will be considered to be the child's.
- Set up a Registered Education Saving Plan (RESP) for your child. Deposits are not deductible, but the Education Savings Grant and any income earned within the plan will be taxable to the child when withdrawn.
- When your child goes off to college or university, consider buying him a home to live in while at school rather than paying the rent. When he graduates, the increase in value of the home will be his gain and will be exempt from tax as his principal residence for each year after he turns 19.

Documents or Information Needed

- Information that shows transfers of assets to the minor child are held in trust and ownership of the funds has been fully transferred.
- Information that confirms the source of the funds in order to properly track who should be reporting the income.

Questions for Your Advisor

- Should I be reporting my child's part-time earnings and filing a tax return?
- Will the investment earnings on birthday money and other gifts my parents give to my children be taxed to me, my children or my parents?
- Should my child be contributing to an Registered Retirement Savings Plan? Is there an over-contribution limit?
- Should my child's earnings be used to contribute to an RESP?
- What is the best way to pay my child for working in my business?
- Should my child be spending his money to fund tuition, or should I be gifting this money to him?

#6 BABYSITTING — WHO CLAIMS WHAT

What You Need to Know

Expenses for the care of dependant children so that you can work or attend school are eligible for the child care expense deduction. This deduction is generally claimable by the lower income spouse, unless that spouse is confined to a bed or wheelchair or is a patient in a hospital or asylum for at least two weeks, disabled on a long-term basis, in prison or like institution for at least two weeks, separated from you for at least 90 days ending in the tax year or attending a designated educational institution.

If amounts are paid to a relative, that relative must be over 17 years old. You cannot pay deductible child care to your spouse.

Child care claims are limited to two-thirds of the earned income of the individual making the claim and may reduce the amount of the child tax credit and the disability supplement for disabled dependants.

Documents or Information Needed
- Receipts for amount paid, including the name (and Social Insurance Number) of the provider
- Form T2201 completed by a physician if you are making a claim for child care expenses for a child with disabilities
- Names and ages of children for whom care was provided
- Dates when low-income spouse was unable to provide care
- Number of weeks the claimant was a student
- If the child is not your child or your spouse's child, the child's income

Questions for Your Advisor
- Can I claim the fees for sending the children to summer camp?
- Can I pay my mother to babysit my children?
- Are nursery school fees deductible? Is it more advantageous to pay a nanny to come to my home?
- Are child care expenses deductible while I search for work?
- Who claims child care expenses in the year of marriage or divorce or when we started living as common-law partners?

#7 DISABILITY AMOUNT — WHO QUALIFIES

What You Need to Know

Taxpayers who suffer from a severe and prolonged disability may be eligible for the disability amount — almost $6,200 in 2002 and an additional amount of about $3,600 for children who are disabled. However, the tax department is strict about who qualifies.

If the individual requires life-sustaining therapy, such as kidney dialysis at least three times per week to an average of at least 14 hours per week, they will also qualify. The disability is considered to be prolonged if it lasts or is expected to last at least 12 months.

The following conditions are considered severe:

- Blindness at any time in the year
- Inability to feed or dress oneself (or situations in which this is possible but only after taking an inordinately long period of time to do so)
- Inability to perform basic functions, even with therapy or the use of devices and medication. These can include the following functions: perceiving, thinking, remembering or other cognitive functions, speaking (or hearing) to be understood by a familiar person in a quiet setting, walking or controlling bowel and/or bladder functions.

If the person with disabilities does not require the amount themselves, it may be transferred to a supporting individual (parent, spouse or other person).

Documents or Information Needed

- Form T2201 (Disability Credit Certificate)
- If transferring the credit, a copy of the person's return for the year

Questions for Your Advisor

- Can cancer patients and Alzheimer's patients qualify for this amount and when?
- Can the tax department refuse to allow this credit once I have qualified for it?
- Can I claim both nursing home fees and the disability amount for my sick spouse?
- Does the fact that I qualify for the Canada Pension Plan Disability benefits automatically qualify me for this disability amount?
- Can I file for an adjustment of my tax return if I missed claiming this credit in the past?
- Can I file for an adjustment if we missed transferring the credit to a supporting individual?

#8 CLAIMING MEDICAL EXPENSES

What You Need to Know

If your medical expenses exceed 3% of your net income, you may claim a credit for them, which is valuable if you are taxable. Generally it is the spouse with the lower net income who makes this claim for maximum benefits. Allowable medical expenses include those outlined below.

Medical Practitioners

- a dentist
- a medical doctor
- a medical practitioner
- an optometrist
- a pharmacist
- a psychologist
- a speech-language pathologist
- an osteopath
- a chiropractor
- a naturopath
- a therapeutist (or therapist)
- a physiotherapist
- a chiropodist (or podiatrist)
- a Christian science practitioner
- a psychoanalyst
- a psychologist
- a qualified speech-language pathologist or audiologist
- an occupational therapist
- an acupuncturist
- a dietician
- a dental hygienist
- a nurse
- an audiologist (after Feb 18, 1997)

Treatments

- medical and dental services
- attendant care
- nursing home care
- ambulance fees
- transportation
- travel expenses
- eyeglasses
- guide dogs
- transplant costs
- alterations to the home for disabled persons
- lip reading or sign language training
- Sign language services
- moving expenses for a disabled person to a more suitable dwelling
- van for wheelchair
- caregiver training
- therapy for a disabled patient
- tutoring services for a patient with a learning disability or mental impairment
- prescribed drugs
- lab tests
- private health plan premiums

Devices

- an artificial limb
- an iron lung
- a rocking bed for poliomyelitis victims
- a wheelchair
- crutches
- a spinal brace
- a brace for a limb
- an ileostomy or a colostomy pad
- a truss for a hernia
- an artificial eye
- a laryngeal speaking aid
- an aid to hearing
- an artificial kidney machine

Documents or Information Needed

- Receipts for all of the devices, procedures, drugs, remodelling, etc.
- Your pay stubs if that is the source of payment of group medical premiums
- Blue Cross or other private health services payments made
- Any medical expenses that were not claimed last year
- Documents verifying any portion of costs not reimbursed as submitted to group plans.

Questions for Your Advisor

- What is the best 12-month period to claim our medical expenses in?
- Which spouse should claim the medical expenses this year?
- Are expenses incurred while abroad tax deductible?
- Can I claim the medical expenses of my children even if they worked?
- How do I adjust my prior-filed returns for missed medical expenses?

#9 GIVING TO CHARITIES

What You Need to Know

Donations to registered charities in Canada are eligible for a two-tiered tax credit. The first $200 is eligible for a credit at the lowest marginal tax rate and the amount above $200 is eligible for a credit at the highest marginal rate. Therefore, it is generally advantageous for one spouse to claim all of the donations, regardless of who made them.

Special tax incentives exist for donations of publicly traded securities acquired via stock options or purchased on the stock market. Ask your advisor for details.

Donations not claimed in the current year may be carried forward and claimed in any of the next five years.

Documents or Information Needed

- Receipts for donations to registered charities in Canada (official receipts will include the charity's registration number)
- Documentation of cost amount for donation of publicly traded securities
- Details of stock options if donating shares acquired through employee stock options
- Receipts for donations to any of the following organizations:
  - Tax-exempt housing corporations resident in Canada
  - Registered Canadian amateur athletic associations
  - Gifts to Canada, a province or municipality or to Her Majesty
  - The United Nations or its agencies
  - Certain universities outside Canada which have received recent donations from the federal government
  - Certain non-profit organizations that only provide low-cost housing to seniors
  - Charities outside Canada to which the Government of Canada has made a donation in the current or previous taxation year
  - Registered national arts service organizations
  - Federal Debt Servicing and Reduction Account
  - US Charities (if you have US source income)

Questions for Your Advisor

- Can we claim the donations made through work as well?
- Did you claim the donations we carried forward from the previous year and should we carry forward donations to next year?
- What is the maximum donation we can make based on our income?
- How much can be donated in the year of death and what is the best way to leave money to charity when I die?

#10 WHAT IF YOU MOVE

What You Need to Know
If you move at least 40 km in order to earn income at the new location or to attend a post-secondary school, you can deduct your moving expenses from your income at the new location. The following expenses are eligible:
- Cost of selling your former residence (e.g. real estate commissions, etc.)
- Costs of keeping a vacant old residence up for sale (to a maximum of $5,000) while you attempt to sell it (e.g. mortgage interest, etc.)
- Expenses of purchasing the new home, including transfer taxes and legal fees (as long as the old home was owned)
- Temporary living expenses (meals and lodging) for up to 15 days
- Removal and storage costs
- Transportation costs and costs of meals on route
- Cost of revising legal documents to show the new address (e.g. replacing drivers licenses, connecting utilities)

If your expenses exceed your income at the new location, you may carry forward your expenses to apply against your income in the following taxation year.

Documents or Information Needed
- Receipts for expenses outlined above
- Distance from old home to new work location and distance from new home to new work location
- Date of move and date you started your new job, business or studies
- Number of household members in the move
- Distance travelled

Questions for Your Advisor
- When is the best time for me to move my family from a tax point of view?
- In which province do I pay the least amount of tax?
- If I move out of Canada temporarily, how does that affect my taxes?
- What happens if I don't have income at the new location until next year?
- How do I deduct expenses of the move that I incur the year after the move?
- Should I take my RRSP deduction this year or save it until next year, given my large moving expense claim?
- What investments should I tap to finance the move?
- Are there capital losses in my carry forward amount to offset capital gains I might generate?

#11 SUPPORT PAYMENTS — CAN THEY BE CLAIMED

What You Need to Know

Support paid by you for the support of your children or your former spouse is deductible if:

- The amounts paid are pursuant to a written separation agreement or court order and that agreement/order has not been changed (in the case of child support, the agreement must have been made prior to May 1, 1997)
- You and your former spouse are separated and living apart at the time of the payments
- Payments are made to your spouse or a third party for the maintenance of the children or former spouse
- Payments are payable on a periodic basis

In the case of child support, a joint election must not have been filed to make the payments tax-free to the recipient.

Payments deductible to the payor are taxable to the recipient. The deduction for support payments reduces your earned income for Registered Retirement Savings Plan (RRSP) purposes. Taxable support payments received increase RRSP earned income of the recipient.

Documents or Information Needed

- Evidence of payments made (receipts or cancelled cheques)
- Copy of separation agreement or court order to determine deductible amount

Questions for Your Advisor

- What is the best time of the year to formalize a separation or divorce from a tax viewpoint?
- Who claims the amount for eligible dependant in the year of break-up and in the year of remarriage or reconciliation?
- How is the Canada Child Tax Benefit affected by the separation?
- Can my legal fees for the divorce, maintenance agreement and its enforcement be claimed as a deduction?
- How are the assets of the union divided and are there any tax consequences?
- Can you prepare tax calculations to show how each party's tax scenario will change when the terms of separation/divorce are implemented?
- What can be done to finalize the support agreements to each party's best tax benefit?
- How will an RRSP contribution help me to reduce income due to the inclusion of the support payments?

#12 HIGHER EDUCATION — HOW TO CLAIM IT

What You Need to Know

Students are eligible to claim tuition fees paid (if at least $100) as well as an education amount of $400 per month for full-time attendance and $120 per month for part-time attendance at a post-secondary institution.

If the student does not need the tuition and education amounts to reduce her taxes to zero, she may transfer the lesser of the unused amount and $5,000 less her claim to a supporting individual. Amounts not used and not transferred may be carried forward for use in subsequent years.

Documents or Information Needed

- Form T2202 or T2202A from the educational institution if claiming the credits for yourself
- Form T2202 or T2202A signed on the back by the student if claiming a transfer of the credits

Questions for Your Advisor

- How much money can my child earn before it hurts my ability to claim tuition and education credits on my return?
- How does scholarship income impact the claim for the tuition/education amount?
- Are the cost of books deductible? What about student fees and board and lodging?
- Can I claim the costs of sending my child to a private high school?
- Are costs of sending a child to a special school for medical reasons deductible?
- Are the costs of tuition for studies abroad deductible here?
- Are moving expenses to attend college in Canada or the US deductible?
- How long can the student carry forward unused tuition/education amounts?
- Did you remember to claim unused amounts from prior years?
- How do payments from the Registered Education Saving Plan we have set up for our child impact our ability to claim tuition and education credits for that child?
- Can Registered Retirement Savings Plan contributions gifted to our child increase our family's chances of claiming tuition and education credits?

#13 EMPLOYMENT EXPENSES

What You Need to Know

If you are required by your employer to pay your own expenses of performing your duties, you may be able to deduct those expenses. Special rules apply to commission salespeople (see #17).

The following expenses are deductible if your employer does not reimburse you or pay you an allowance which is included in your income (i.e. shown on your T4):

- Automobile expenses (see #14)
- Food and beverages
- Home office expenses, office rent and supplies (see #18)
- Salary paid to an assistant
- Telephone expenses — cell phone airtime, long distance calls, internet access
- Travel and lodging expenses while away from your metropolitan area on business for at least 12 hours
- Uniforms (but not clothing that could be worn while not working)

Other costs related to your employment that are deductible include annual union, professional or like dues, legal fees to collect salary or wages owed or severance pay or a retiring allowance.

Documents or Information Needed

- Signed Form T2200 (Declaration of Conditions of Employment) signed
- Auto log and details of automobile expenses (see #14)
- Receipts for expenses listed above
- Home office expenses (see #18)

Questions for Your Advisor

- Can I claim the expenses listed above if my commission income will not arrive until next year?
- What are the tax consequences of buying or leasing my assets, including my car, laptop or phone?
- Should I claim depreciation on my home?
- How do my expenses impact my RRSP deduction?
- Can I ask my employer to reduce my tax withholding charges from my pay cheque if I claim these employment expenses?
- Can I deduct fines and penalties I incur in the course of doing my duties?

#14 AUTOMOBILE EXPENSES

What You Need to Know

Two groups of individuals may claim automobile expenses: employees who are required by the terms of their employment to use their own automobile to earn employment income and self-employed individuals who use an automobile to earn income from self-employment.

The following are possible deductible automobile expenses:
- fuel, tires, maintenance and repairs
- lease payments and interest costs on loan to purchase automobile
- insurance, license and registration
- auto club
- car washes and parking

Documents or Information Needed

Employees
- Form T2200 (Declaration of Conditions of Employment) — signed by your employer
- Receipts for all expenses (except car washes and parking meters)
- Auto log detailing the beginning and ending odometer reading and purpose of each trip. See sample format on next page
- Amount of any reimbursement received from your employer that was not included in income

Self-employed
- Receipts for all expenses (except car washes and parking meters)
- Auto log detailing the beginning and ending odometer reading and purpose of each trip. See sample format on next page

Other
- Details of any automobile purchases, sales or trade-ins in the year

Auto Log

Business:_____   Tax Year:_____

Date	km Start	km Finish	Destination	Reason for Trip	Gas/Oil	M&R	Wash	Park	Other

Distance: **Totals:**

Questions for Your Advisor
- Do I qualify to claim automobile expenses against employment income?
- How do I qualify to make this claim in the future?
- What are the tax implications of using an employer-provided car that is leased or owned by the employer?
- What are the tax implications of receiving an allowance to cover auto expenses?
- What is the best way to record personal use driving?
- Is driving to and from my place of work tax deductible?

#15 ENTERTAINMENT EXPENSES

What You Need to Know

Entertainment expenses are deductible by employees who are compensated, at least in part, by commissions and by self-employed individuals. In most cases your deduction will be 50% of the amount paid.

Entertainment expenses include the costs of the following items if they relate to entertainment of associates, staff, assistants, clients or potential clients you work with in the course of earning self-employment or commission income:

- cruises
- entertaining at athletic or sporting clubs
- entertaining while on vacation or similar trips
- hospitality suites
- meals and beverages
- security escorts
- taxes, gratuities and cover charges
- tickets to the theatre, concerts, fashion shows or athletic events
- tour guides

Documents or Information Needed

- Records of the names and business addresses of the customers or other persons being entertained, together with the relevant places, dates, times and amounts supported by such vouchers as are reasonably obtainable

Questions for Your Advisor

- Can I claim the costs of my own meals when I travel out of town?
- Are there any exceptions to the 50% restriction for meals and entertainment costs?
- When can entertainment costs be considered promotional in nature?
- How are memberships to and entertaining at private clubs, golf clubs deducted?

#16 SEVERANCE & RETIRING ALLOWANCES

What You Need to Know
Upon termination of your employment, it is common to receive a severance package or retiring allowance. When you receive a retiring allowance, it will generally be reported on a T4A Slip.

A portion of the retiring allowance will be designated as eligible and a portion as ineligible. This refers to whether or not you can transfer or roll over the amounts to a tax-deferred savings plan:

Eligible means that the amount can be transferred to a Registered Pension Plan (RPP) or a Registered Retirement Savings Plan (RRSP) without being included in your income or using up any of your RRSP contribution room. This eligible amount can only be transferred to your RRSP, not your spouse's.

Ineligible means that portion designated as such may be contributed to your RRSP if you have unused contribution room. You have the option of contributing it to a spousal RRSP as well.

Documents or Information Needed
- T4A Slip
- Receipts for RRSP contributions

Questions for Your Advisor
- What will my tax liability be if I do not contribute any of my retiring allowance to an RRSP or RPP?
- What is the best tax advantage I can receive under the rules for RRSP roll-overs and top-ups?
- How will my RRSP deduction affect other provisions on the tax return in the year of job termination?
- Can I avoid a clawback of my Employment Insurance benefits by making this RRSP contribution? Or increase my Child Tax Benefit or GST/HST Credit?
- Should I use the money to buy another RRSP, a Labour-Sponsored Investment Fund, pay down my mortgage or contribute to a Registered Education Savings Plan for my child or grandchild?
- If I use the tax savings to fund a new business or consulting venture, how can my start-up costs provide a tax benefit to me?
- How much tax will I have to pay if I need to withdraw money from my RRSP to live, if I can't find a job right away?

#17 COMMISSION SALES — CLAIMING EXPENSES

What You Need to Know
If you are an employee you may claim sales expenses if you earn at least part of your income as commission from sales or negotiating contracts for your employer and you are required to perform your duties away from your employer's place of business and to pay your own expenses.

Claims may be made under two different sets of rules. Your advisor will determine your best option based on the information you present.

Documents or Information Needed
- Signed Form T2200 (Declaration of Conditions of Employment), indicating compliance with the conditions noted above
- Auto log and details of automobile expenses (see #14)
- Receipts for accounting fees to organize or maintain your expense records
- Receipts for legal expenses
- Receipts for other travel expenses such as air, bus, or train travel
- Receipts for supplies used directly in your work
- Record of salary expenses of an assistant
- Receipts for office rent
- Details of workspace for in the home expenses (see #18)
- Details of entertainment expenses (see #15)

Note that employees may not claim the costs of buying a computer, cell phone or assets other than an automobile, musical instrument or aircraft used for employment purposes. If you need a computer or cell phone, consider renting them if the after-tax cost is less than buying.

Questions for Your Advisor
- Should I claim based on the few receipts I have remembered to keep for my auto expenses or can I make a "cents per kilometre claim"?
- Do you need a record of my trips out of town?
- Are tips included in the deductible costs? How do I account for expenses for which I have no receipts (car washes, parking meters, telephones)?
- Can I claim the costs of hiring my spouse or child as my assistant?
- What receipts should be kept to claim legal costs and supply costs?

#18 HOME WORKSPACE EXPENSES

What You Need to Know
If you use a portion of your home exclusively to earn income from a business or, as an employee, are required by your employer to have an office in your home, you may be eligible to claim your expenses for maintaining that office.

The following are expenses that may be eligible for home workspace, depending on your source of income (employment, employed commission sales, self-employed): electricity and heat, insurance, maintenance, mortgage interest and property taxes.

Home workspace expenses cannot be used to create or increase a loss from the source of income against which they are claimed. Unused home workspace expenses may be carried forward to be claimed against income in future years, however, so you'll need to provide this carry-forward information to your tax pro next year.

Documents or Information Needed
- Receipts for all expenditures including utilities, repairs, maintenance, supplies
- Sketch of your home indicating the area used as a home workspace
- Area of your home used as a home workspace
- Total living area of your home

Questions for your Advisor
- Is driving to and from my home office tax deductible?
- Am I able to use last year's home office expenses this year?
- Can I claim the cost of replacing my roof or putting in new carpets?
- How do I deduct the furniture, communications equipment and servicing costs I have for my home office?
- Can I write off common area space use like bathrooms and hallways?
- Are my cleaning expenses tax deductible?
- What happens, for tax filing purposes, when both spouses are self-employed and use the same office space at different times of the day?
- If the home is used in a babysitting enterprise, how are home office expenses calculated, if the children use up most of the home in daily activities?

#19 SELF-EMPLOYED — WHAT'S INCOME & WHAT'S DEDUCTIBLE

What You Need to Know

When you operate a business, you must report the income you earn each year, even if you do not receive it in the year. That's called the accrual method of accounting. Only farmers and small cash-based businesses may use the cash method of reporting income. Self-employment income includes the following:

- Sales
- Commissions
- Fees
- Barter transactions

The following expenses are common deductible expenses of a business with a reasonable expectation of profit:

- Accounting fees
- Advertising
- Automobile expenses (see #14)
- Business licenses
- Business taxes
- Cost of goods sold
- Delivery
- Dues and memberships
- Entertainment expenses
- Freight
- Fuel
- Home workspace expenses (see #18)
- Insurance
- Legal fees
- Maintenance and repairs
- Management and administration fees
- Meals
- Office expenses
- Private health care premiums
- Professional fees
- Property taxes
- Rent
- Salaries, wages and benefits
- Supplies
- Telephone
- Travel
- Utilities

Capital expenditures, those made to acquire income-producing assets like buildings, furniture and fixtures, vehicles, etc., may be depreciated if the asset has a useful life of more than one year.

In the case of an unincorporated small business, it is the net income that is subject to taxation on the personal tax return. Business owners who are required to collect and remit GST/HST are eligible to receive a GST/HST rebate paid on all expenses.

Documents or Information Needed
- Record of all income
- Record of all operating expenses
- Business journal (see sample below). This is the place to record the names of clients and activities pursued to earn income; your auto log and unreceipted expense log. This is a critical tool in winning a tax audit.

Daily Business Journal

Business:_____   **Date:**_____

Time	To Do	Incoming Items	Follow-up	Expense Details
6:00 am				
7:00 am				
8:00 am				
9:00 am				

Questions for Your Advisor
- Can I hire my spouse or minor children and deduct their wages?
- How do I account for expenses that have some personal use component?
- How do I justify a loss in my business to the tax department?
- How can I use my loss to recover taxes paid from prior years?
- Can I adjust my tax return if I forgot to claim expenses or capital cost allowance in the past?

#20 RENTAL INCOME — WHAT'S DEDUCTIBLE

What You Need to Know

You must report rental income received if there is a profit motive involved. If you charge a family member rent in order to defer some of the costs of providing accommodation, you need not report the rental income.

The following expenses may be deducted if they are incurred in order to earn rental income:

- Advertising, office expenses (stationery, postage, etc.)
- Property taxes and insurance, maintenance and repairs and utilities
- Motor vehicle costs, if you operate two or more rental properties (see #14)
- Legal, accounting and other professional fees
- Salaries, wages and benefits paid to employees

You may also claim depreciation on the building and any furniture, fixtures or equipment, but be aware that if your sell the property for more than you paid to acquire it, you will have to include these amounts in your income (recapture) in the year you sell the property.

Documents or Information Needed

- Record of all rents received, including a tenant log, vacancy log; and justification of fair market value of rent charged and the reasonable expectation of profit
- Receipts for all expenses, including details of all improvements
- Name and address of each owner of the property and their relationship to one another
- Details of the acquisition; relationship of the buyer to the vendor
- Purpose of acquiring the property
- Financing details, interest and principal repayment schedules
- When you dispose of the property you'll need: a record of costs of acquiring the property, a record of the cost of all improvements made to the property while you owned it and details of the proceeds of disposal and all expenses relating to the sale

Questions for Your Advisor

- How are refinancing charges or mortgage penalty fees treated for tax purposes?
- Can I hire my spouse or child to help with maintenance and repairs and deduct the expenses of the salaries I pay?
- What happens if I convert my rental property into a personal property and vice versa?
- What are the tax consequences if the property is repossessed?

#21 INVESTMENT EXPENSES — WHAT'S DEDUCTIBLE

What You Need to Know
In order for these costs to be deductible, there must be the possibility that the investment will generate investment income — that is interest, dividends or rental income. If the only possible return on your investment is from capital gains on its sale, your investment costs may not be deductible.

Carrying charges relating to registered investments, such as your Registered Retirement Savings Plan (RRSP), are not deductible although the costs of borrowing to top up your Registered Pension Plan (RPP) may be deducted as RPP contributions. Discuss these points with your tax advisor.

Note that interest paid on money borrowed to invest will continue to be deductible even if the investment principal is lost. However, these rules generally do not apply to the loss in value of a real property or depreciable property.

Documents or Information Needed
- Safety deposit box rental receipt
- Accounting fee receipt for recording/organizing your investment information
- Investment counsel fees
- Interest paid on employer-provided loans
- T4 Slip: the taxable benefit of a low-interest loan from employers if the money was used to purchase investments
- Interest paid on Canada Savings Bonds purchased on payroll deduction
- Interest paid on life insurance policy loans
- Management and safe custody fees for non-registered investments
- Interest paid on loans for investment purposes
- Details of any non-investment use of funds borrowed
- Loan agreements with your spouse and details of repayments amounts

Questions for Your Advisor
- How are deductible interest costs computed when I use my line of credit for investment purposes?
- Are my interest costs deductible if I borrow money to buy assets I will be transferring to my spouse or child?
- When is mortgage interest paid tax deductible?
- How are my interest deduction costs affected by systematic withdrawals out of my mutual fund accounts?

#22 MUTUAL FUNDS & CAPITAL GAINS OR LOSSES

What You Need to Know

There are three numbers needed to calculate your capital gain on the disposition of your mutual fund units held outside a registered account. These numbers are the *adjusted cost base*, the *proceeds of disposition* and the *outlays and expenses*.

Mutual fund units are treated as identical properties, meaning that one unit in a given fund is the same as any other unit in that fund. You may have acquired your units by purchasing them or as a result of re-investment of earnings from the fund.

When you dispose of your identical properties, unless you dispose of all of them, the ones disposed of are deemed to be *average* properties. An average cost is subtracted from the proceeds of disposition to arrive at your capital gain or loss. Rather than keeping track of *when* they were acquired, it is important to track the *cost* at which they were acquired or re-invested. You'll need to track this manually from all your statements or have the mutual fund company provide you with this information.

When you switch from one fund to another, the switch has two tax consequences: a disposition is considered to be made of the first units at the current market value and the capital cost of the replacement units is recorded at that same value. Such dispositions must be reported in the year that they occur.

Documents or Information Needed
- Confirmation statements for all purchases of units and slips for each sale of units
- Statements for each income re-investment
- Record of any elections made regarding these units (Form T664 from 1994)
- Record of all loans taken to buy mutual fund units and interest paid thereon
- Exchange rate at time of each transaction in foreign currency

Questions for Your Advisor
- What is the adjusted cost base of each of my mutual fund holdings?
- How do dividend reinvestment programs change the cost base of my mutual fund holdings?
- When is the best time to generate gains or losses for tax purposes?
- Do I have any capital losses from prior years that will offset my capital gains this year?
- Will my borrowing costs be deductible under tax advantaged funds that pay me a portion of my capital back as income?

#23 SHARES & CAPITAL GAINS OR LOSSES

What You Need to Know
Shares of publicly traded corporations, held outside your registered accounts, are treated as identical properties (as described under #22). The adjusted cost base of shares of privately held corporations are treated the same way.

However, two types of shares differ in the tax calculation of losses that result on disposition. Losses from the disposition of *privately held* shares of a small business corporation are considered to be business investment losses, deductible against other income. Allowable losses from the sale of *publicly traded* shares may only be used to offset other capital gains of the year.

They also differ in the calculation of capital gains: gains on the disposition of shares from a qualified small business corporation may qualify for the $500,000 capital gains deduction.

Documents or Information Needed
- Broker's confirmation for all purchases of the stock and slips for each sale
- Record of any elections made regarding these shares (Form T664 from 1994)
- Carry forward record of any prior year use of your lifetime capital gains deduction
- Exchange rate at time of purchase or sale if transactions in foreign currency
- Dates and split or consolidation ratios while you owned the shares. Stock splits will not be reported but will affect the calculation of your cost base.

Questions for Your Advisor
- What information is required to account for my adjusted cost base of assets?
- How does a capital gains election made in 1994 affect my tax status?
- Can I transfer my capital gain to my lower earning spouse?
- How are capital losses claimed for each type of capital property I own?
- What is my unrealized capital gain or loss in my investment portfolio and when should each be generated?

#24 PERSONAL PROPERTY & CAPITAL GAINS OR LOSSES

What You Need to Know

Personal use property is a special class of capital property that includes your personal cars, boats and vacation property. Some personal properties that increase in value are included in *listed personal property*, to which additional rules apply and consists of items like jewellery, art, rare books and stamps held for personal use and enjoyment which normally increase in value.

A special rule applies for low-cost items. The cost of the asset and the proceeds of disposition must amount to at least $1,000 — no need to report small transactions. When the property consists of a collection, the $1,000 rule applies to the whole collection, not to individual items. Special rules apply if you owned the property before 1972 or if the property is acquired after February 27, 2000, as part of a charitable donation scheme.

One-half of the gain on the disposition of personal use or listed personal property is taxable.

Losses on the properties are treated differently, however. Personal use property losses are considered to be personal living expenses and are not deductible. This includes losses on your personal residences. If you lose money on listed personal property, you may only deduct your losses against gains on other listed personal property in the current year, in the preceding three years or those gains incurred in the future.

Documents or Information Needed

- Evidence of purchase of the item or the value of the item when it was acquired
- Costs of any additions (if a collection) or improvements (e.g. to a cottage)
- Bill of sale
- If you pre-reported capital gains in 1994, a copy of Form T664
- Outlays and expenses to dispose of the property (such as real estate commissions)

Questions for Your Advisor

- Do I have to report the transfer of my cottage to my spouse or children?
- How do I determine the value of property I wish to transfer to family members or that were transferred to me?
- How is the transfer of my property handled in case of my death or divorce?
- How is the disposition of my property treated when I hold back a mortgage on the property?

#25 PRINCIPAL RESIDENCE & CAPITAL GAINS OR LOSSES

What You Need to Know

Under current tax rules, each family is allowed to have one tax-exempt principal residence. Prior to 1982, each spouse was allowed to have one tax-exempt principal residence.

If you own more than one residence, you can designate one each year as your principal residence. When you sell or otherwise dispose of one of your residences, your tax professional must calculate the exempt portion of any gain.

If you change the use of your principal residence to some other purpose (such as renting out a portion of it), you can deem that the change in use be ignored as long as you do not claim capital cost allowance (depreciation) on the property.

If you are designating a property as your principal residence for each year you owned it, the capital gain is completely exempt and you do not need to provide the details listed below.

Documents or Information Needed

- Statement of Adjustments and other documents provided by your lawyer when you purchased the property and when you sold it
- Record of all additions and improvements to the property
- Record of any elections made regarding this property (Form T664 from 1994)
- Details of any partial dispositions such as appropriations or subdivisions
- Which years you wish to designate this property as your principal residence
- Value of the property at the end of 1981
- The value of the property when you inherited it or when you transferred it to your spouse, child or others

Questions for Your Advisor

- How long do I have to live in my property to designate it as a principal residence?
- Can I designate my condo in the US as a principal residence? Are there US tax consequences?
- Can I buy a principal residence for my adult children as a gift?
- What are the tax consequences if the financial institution forecloses on my mortgage?
- What does tax loss selling mean and how can I use this option to my advantage?
- Are there any losses to carry forward to offset this year's taxable gains or should losses of the current year be carried back to offset prior year gains?

#26 REAL PROPERTY & CAPITAL GAINS OR LOSSES

What You Need to Know
The adjusted cost base of real property consists not only of the purchase price of the property, but also most other costs of acquiring the property. It also includes the costs of any improvements you make to the property while you own it. Be sure to keep a record of these expenditures each year and bring them to your tax advisor when you sell or otherwise dispose of the property.

Documents or Information Needed
- Statement of Adjustments and other documents provided by your lawyer when you purchased the property and when you sold it
- Allocation of value between land and building at time of purchase
- Record of all additions or improvements to the property while you owned it
- Exchange rate at time of each transaction in foreign currency
- Details of any partial dispositions such as appropriations or subdivisions
- Record of any elections made regarding this property (Form T664 from 1994)

Questions for Your Advisor
- How are real property transactions treated in the case of emigration, death, divorce, transfer of property to children or other third parties and remarriage?
- What is the difference between an improvement to the property and a repair (which is fully deductible)?
- Can my travel costs in driving to collect rents or repair properties be deducted?
- What expenses of the sale are deductible and which are used to reduce the capital gain?
- How are the gains/losses of co-owners handled?
- What are the tax consequences when a building is sold for more than its undepreciated cost?
- When should capital cost allowance be taken as a deduction to reduce income?

#27 YOUR FARM & CAPITAL GAINS OR LOSSES

What You Need to Know
Gains on the disposition of a qualified farm property are eligible for an exemption of up to $500,000.

A qualified farm property is property owned by you or a family farm partnership in which you hold an interest and includes property that satisfies one of the following conditions:
- A share of the capital stock of a family farm corporation that you or your spouse own
- An interest in a family farm partnership that you or your spouse own
- Real property (land or buildings) or eligible capital property

Real property or eligible capital property is qualified farm property only if it is used in carrying on a farming business in Canada by you or your spouse, any of your children, any of your parents, a family farm corporation where any of these individuals own a share of the corporation or a family farm partnership where any of these individuals own an interest in the partnership.

Documents or Information Needed
- Documentation regarding the cost of the property. If acquired by bequest, a copy of the final return of the former owner may be required
- Documentation for the cost of any additions or improvements to the property
- Documentation for the proceeds of disposition and any outlays and expenses relating to disposing of the property
- Form T664 (Capital Gains Election from 1994)

Questions for Your Advisor
- Does our property qualify for the $500,000 capital gains deduction?
- Are there any restrictions to the use of this deduction?
- How does the capital gains election we made in 1994 affect this deduction?
- What other provisions on the tax return will be affected by this disposition?
- How can I best use the deduction now to minimize my taxes at death?
- Is an estate freeze the answer to tax savings in the future?
- Can I claim this deduction if I am emigrating from Canada?

#28 SMALL BUSINESS SHARES & CAPITAL GAINS OR LOSSES

What You Need to Know
Gains on the disposition of qualified small business corporation shares are eligible for an exemption of up to $500,000.

Qualified small business corporation shares are shares in a Canadian-controlled private corporation (CCPC) in which all or most (90% or more) of the fair market value of its assets satisfy one of the following conditions:
- Used mainly in an active business, carried on primarily in Canada by the corporation or by a related corporation
- Shares or debts of connected corporations that were small business corporations
- A combination of these two types of assets

To qualify, the shares must meet the following criteria:
- Throughout the 24 months immediately before disposition, no one other than you, or a person or partnership related to you, owned the share
- Throughout the 24 months immediately before disposition, while the shares were owned by you, or a person or partnership related to you, it was a share of a CCPC of which more than 50% of the fair market value of the assets were used mainly in an active business carried on primarily in Canada by the CCPC, or by a related corporation, certain shares or debts of connected corporations or a combination of these two types of assets.

Documents or Information Needed
- Documentation regarding the cost of the property. If acquired by bequest, a copy of the final return of the former owner may be required
- Documentation for the cost of any additions or improvements to the property
- Documentation for the proceeds of disposition and any outlays and expenses relating to disposing of the property
- Form T664 (Capital Gains Election from 1994)

Questions for Your Advisor
- Do our shares qualify for the $500,000 capital gains deduction?
- Are there any restrictions to the use of this deduction?
- How does the capital gains election we made in 1994 affect this deduction?
- What other provisions on the tax return will be affected by this disposition?
- How can I best use the deduction now to minimize my taxes at death?
- Is an estate freeze the answer to tax savings in the future?
- Can I claim this deduction if I am emigrating from Canada?

#29 SAVING FOR YOUR CHILD'S EDUCATION (RESP)

What You Need to Know

Investments in Registered Education Savings Plans (RESP) have no tax consequences until the funds are withdrawn from the plan, either by the beneficiary in order to fund post-secondary education or by the contributor.

When you make a contribution to an RESP for a minor child, a tax-free Canada Education Savings Grant (CESG) will be generated — a grant of 20% for up to $2,000 contributed. The earnings on the CESG and the RESP contribution accumulate on a tax-deferred basis.

However, when withdrawing funds, the following special rules apply:
- When amounts are withdrawn, original contributions are returned to the contributor tax free (since they were not deductible when contributed)
- If the beneficiary uses the fund for post-secondary education, the accumulated income and CESGs are included in the student's income in the year they are received
- If the beneficiary does not attend a post-secondary institution the CESG is returned to the government by the trustee and the accumulated earnings in the account are taxable to the contributor but may be transferred (to a maximum of $50,000) to his own or to a spousal Registered Retirement Savings Plan (RRSP). Amounts not transferred are reported on a T4A Slip and are subject to an additional 20% tax in addition to the taxes normally calculated on the income.

Documents or Information Needed

- Available CESG room: up to $2,000 per year and the room can be carried forward.
- Form T1171 (Tax Withholding Waiver on Accumulated Income Payments from RESPs) to ensure no tax is withheld on the transfer of an RESP balance to a contributor's RRSP

Questions for Your Advisor

- Is the RESP a good investment for our family or should we contribute to our RRSP or a Labour-Sponsored Investment Fund instead?
- Should our Child Tax Benefits be invested in the RESP?
- What are the penalty taxes if the beneficiary does not go to school and the money is withdrawn by the contributor?
- How much can be withdrawn from the RESP to fund schooling in the first year?
- How can RRSP planning be used to maximize education funding?

#30 SAVING FOR YOUR RETIREMENT (RRSP)

What You Need to Know

Each year, your Registered Retirement Savings Plan (RRSP) contribution room (the amount you are eligible to contribute) is calculated — 18% of your earned income in the previous taxation year to a maximum of $13,500 for tax years 1996 to 2003, $14,500 in 2004, $15,500 in 2005. Those amounts will be indexed thereafter.

This contribution room is carried forward each year and is reduced by your pension adjustment (see your T4 Slip) and by your actual RRSP contributions made. Your unused RRSP contribution room is shown on the Notice of Assessment or Reassessment you receive each year from the tax department (CCRA). Note:

- Contributions based on your available contribution room may be made to your own RRSP or to your spouse's RRSP.
- Your RRSP deduction reduces net income and therefore, in addition to reducing your taxes, it may have the following side effects which will increase the money in your pocket: increased GST/HST Credit, Canada Child Tax Benefit (CCTB), age amount, provincial tax credits and decreased Employment Insurance (EI) repayment and Old Age Security (OAS) clawback.
- Contributions may be made during the taxation year or within 60 days after the end of the taxation year.
- Contributions made in a given year need not be deducted that year but may be deducted in a subsequent year.
- If you contribute more than $2,000 more than your limit, the excess contributions are subject to a special tax of 1% per month until they are withdrawn from the plan.
- Amounts withdrawn from your RRSP are taxable (unless withdrawn under the Home Buyers' Plan or the Lifelong Learning Plan or transferred to another RRSP, Registered Retirement Investment Fund (RRIF) or a life annuity).
- Withdrawals from a spousal RRSP are taxable to the spouse if no contributions have been made in the current or previous two taxation years. Otherwise, the withdrawals are taxable to the contributor.
- In the year before you turn 70, you must close your RRSP. Funds may be withdrawn (and therefore added to your income), transferred to a RRIF or used to purchase an annuity.

Documents or Information Needed
- RRSP contribution receipts for all contributions
- T4RSPs detailing all withdrawals
- Last year's Notice of Assessment or Reassessment to show your RRSP contribution room
- You should be sure to file a tax return for each year since 1990 to have an accurate unused RRSP contribution room figure

Questions for Your Advisor
- How much money will I save by making an RRSP contribution this year?
- How much more will I receive from CCTB if I make a contribution?
- Can I split my RRSP accumulations with my spouse in retirement?
- How can I use my RRSP funds to buy a home or go to school?
- What happens if I over-contribute to my RRSP?

The T1 General Return (2002)

Canada Customs
and Revenue Agency   Agence des douanes
et du revenu du Canada

T1 GENERAL 2002

Income Tax and Benefit Return

Identification

7

Attach your personal label here. Correct any wrong information.
If you are not attaching a label, print your name and address below.

First name and initial

Last name

Mailing address: Apt. No. – Street No. Street name

P.O. Box, R.R.

City   Prov./Terr.   Postal code

Information about you

Enter your social insurance number (SIN) if it is not on the label, or if you are not attaching a label:

Enter your date of birth: Year   Month   Day

Your language of correspondence: English   Français
Votre langue de correspondance :

Check the box that applies to your marital status on December 31, 2002:
(see the "Marital status" section in the guide for details)

1 ☐ Married   2 ☐ Living common law   3 ☐ Widowed
4 ☐ Divorced   5 ☐ Separated   6 ☐ Single

Information about your spouse or common-law partner (if you checked box 1 or 2 above)

Enter his or her SIN if it is not on the label, or if you are not attaching a label:

Enter his or her first name:

Enter his or her net income for 2002 to claim certain credits: (see the guide for details)

Check this box if he or she was self-employed in 2002:   1 ☐

Information about your residence

Enter your province or territory of residence on **December 31, 2002:**

Enter the province or territory where you **currently** reside if it is not the same as that shown above for your mailing address:

If you were self-employed in 2002, enter the province or territory of self-employment:

If you became or ceased to be a resident of Canada **in 2002**, give the date of:

	Month	Day			Month	Day
entry			or	departure		

If this return is for a deceased person, enter the date of death: Year   Month   Day

Do not use this area

Elections Canada (Canadian citizens only; see the guide for details)

Do you authorize the Canada Customs and Revenue Agency to provide your name, address, and date of birth to Elections Canada for the **National Register of Electors**? .... Yes ☐ 1   No ☐ 2
Your authorization is needed each year. This information will be used for electoral purposes only.

Goods and services tax/harmonized sales tax (GST/HST) credit application

See the guide for details.
Are you applying for the GST/HST credit? .... Yes ☐ 1   No ☐ 2

Your guide contains valuable information to help you complete your return.

When you come to a line on the return that applies to you, look up the line number in the guide for more information.

| Do not use this area | 172 | | | | 171 | | | | |

5000-R

2

Please answer the following question

Did you own or hold foreign property at any time in 2002 with a total cost of more than
CAN$100,000? (read the "Foreign income" section in the guide for details). . . . . 266 Yes ☐ 1   No ☐ 2
If *yes,* attach a completed Form T1135.

If you had certain dealings with a non-resident trust or corporation in 2002, see the "Foreign income" section in the guide.

As a Canadian resident, you have to report your income from all sources both inside and outside Canada.

Total income

Employment income (box 14 on all T4 slips)	101	
Commissions included on line 101 (box 42 on all T4 slips) 102		
Other employment income	104 +	
Old Age Security pension (box 18 on the T4A(OAS) slip)	113 +	
CPP or QPP benefits (box 20 on the T4A(P) slip)	114 +	
Disability benefits included on line 114 (box 16 on the T4A(P) slip) 152		
Other pensions or superannuation	115 +	
Employment Insurance and other benefits (box 14 on the T4E slip)	119 +	
Taxable amount of dividends from taxable Canadian corporations (see the guide)	120 +	
Interest and other investment income (attach Schedule 4)	121 +	
Net partnership income: limited or non-active partners only (attach Schedule 4)	122 +	
Rental income Gross 160 Net 126 +		
Taxable capital gains (attach Schedule 3)	127 +	
Support payments received Total 156 Taxable amount 128 +		
RRSP income (from all T4RSP slips)	129 +	
Other income Specify:	130 +	
Self-employment income (see lines 135 to 143 in the guide)		
Business income Gross 162 Net 135 +		
Professional income Gross 164 Net 137 +		
Commission income Gross 166 Net 139 +		
Farming income Gross 168 Net 141 +		
Fishing income Gross 170 Net 143 +		
Workers' compensation benefits (box 10 on the T5007 slip) 144		
Social assistance payments	145 +	
Net federal supplements (box 21 on the T4A(OAS) slip) 146 +		
Add lines 144, 145, and 146 = ▶ 147 +		
Add lines 101, 104 to 143, and 147		
This is your **total income**. 150 =		

↖ **Attach your completed Schedule 1 and Form 428 here.** **3**
Also attach here any other schedules, information slips, forms, receipts, and
documents that you need to include with your return.

Net income

Enter your **total income** from line 150	150	

Pension adjustment (box 52 on all T4 slips and box 34 on all T4A slips)	206	

Registered pension plan deduction (box 20 on all T4 slips and box 32 on all T4A slips)	207	
RRSP deduction (see Schedule 7; attach receipts)	208 +	
Saskatchewan Pension Plan deduction (maximum $600)	209 +	

Annual union, professional, or like dues (box 44 on all T4 slips, or from receipts)	212 +	
Child care expenses (attach Form T778)	214 +	
Attendant care expenses	215 +	

Business investment loss	Gross **228**	Allowable deduction 217 +	
Moving expenses		219 +	

Support payments made	Total **230**	Allowable deduction 220 +	
Carrying charges and interest expenses (attach Schedule 4)		221 +	
Deduction for CPP or QPP contributions on self-employment and other earnings (attach Schedule 8)		222 +	•
Exploration and development expenses (attach Form T1229)		224 +	
Other employment expenses		229 +	
Clergy residence deduction (attach Form T1223)		231 +	
Other deductions Specify:		232 +	
Add lines 207 to 224, 229, 231, and 232.	233 =	► –	
Line 150 minus line 233 (if negative, enter "0"). This is your **net income before adjustments**.	234 =		

Social benefits repayment (if you reported income on line 113, 119, or 146, see line 235 in the guide)	235 –	•
Line 234 minus line 235 (if negative, enter "0"). If you have a spouse or common-law partner, see line 236 in the guide. This is your **net income**.	236 =	

Taxable income

Employee home relocation loan deduction (box 37 on all T4 slips)	248	
Stock option and shares deductions	249 +	

Other payments deduction (if you reported income on line 147, see line 250 in the guide)	250 +	
Limited partnership losses of other years	251 +	
Non-capital losses of other years	252 +	
Net capital losses of other years	253 +	
Capital gains deduction	254 +	
Northern residents deductions (attach Form T2222)	255 +	
Additional deductions Specify:	256 +	
Add lines 248 to 256.	257 =	► –
Line 236 minus line 257 (if negative, enter "0") This is your **taxable income**.	260 =	

Use your taxable income to calculate your federal tax on Schedule 1.

Refund or Balance owing   **4**

Net federal tax: Enter the amount from line 19 of Schedule 1 (attach Schedule 1 even if the result is "0")		420	
CPP contributions payable on self-employment and other earnings (from Schedule 8)		421 +	
Social benefits repayment (enter the amount from line 235)		422 +	

Provincial or territorial tax (attach Form 428 even if the result is "0")   428 +

Add lines 420 to 428
This is your **total payable**. 435 =   •

Total income tax deducted (from all information slips)	437	•
Refundable Quebec abatement	440 +	•
CPP overpayment (enter your excess contributions)	448 +	•
Employment Insurance overpayment (enter your excess contributions)	450 +	•
Refundable medical expense supplement	452 +	•
Refund of investment tax credit (attach Form T2038(IND))	454 +	•
Part XII.2 trust tax credit (box 38 on all T3 slips)	456 +	•
Employee and partner GST/HST rebate (attach Form GST370)	457 +	•
Tax paid by instalments	476 +	•

Provincial or territorial credits (attach Form 479 if it applies)   479 +   •

Add lines 437 to 479
These are your **total credits**. 482 =   ▶ –

Line 435 minus line 482   =

If the result is negative, you have a **refund**.
If the result is positive, you have a **balance owing**.
Enter the amount below on whichever line applies.

We do not charge or refund a difference of less than $2.

Refund 484 _____   •   **Balance owing** 485 _____   •

▨ **Direct deposit – Start or change** (see line 484 in the guide)

You do not have to complete this area every year. Do not complete it this year
if your direct deposit information for your refund has not changed.

Refund and GST/HST credit – To start direct deposit or to change account
information only, attach a "void" cheque or complete lines 460, 461, and 462.

Note: To deposit your **CCTB** payments (including certain related provincial or
territorial payments) into the **same** account, also check box 463.

Branch number	Institution number	Account number	CCTB
460 _____	461 ____	462 _____	463 ▢
(5 digits)	(3 digits)	(maximum 12 digits)	

Amount enclosed 486 ▢   •

Attach to page 1 a **cheque** or **money order**
payable to the Receiver General. Your payment
is due no later than April 30, 2003.

I certify that the information given on this return and in any documents attached is correct, complete, and fully discloses all my income.	490 **For professional tax preparers only.**	Name: Address:
Sign here _____		
It is a serious offence to make a false return.		
Telephone ( ) Date		Telephone: ( )
Do not use this area 487 ▢ 488 ▢		•

Index

(continued)

About the Author

Throughout her varied career, Evelyn Jacks has established a nationwide reputation as an award-winning entrepreneur, a consistently best-selling author, speaker, educator and publisher in the tax preparation and financial services industries. Evelyn has written 30 books on the subject of personal taxation, as well as over 70 certificate continuing education courses for tax accountants and financial planners.

Evelyn is the President of The Knowledge Bureau, a national company which specializes in intellectual property development and delivery of keynotes, workshops, seminars, trade publications and multi-media broadcasts on the subjects of personal wealth and health, by recognized experts in the financial services and medical industries.

Evelyn's numerous trade publications, including *Make Sure It's Deductible*, have become annual best sellers in Canada over the last 15 years. New are *Tax Secrets in Tough Times*, which focuses on the tax savings opportunities for those experiencing major personal and financial changes and *The 30-Minute Tax Solution*, which provides seven steps for smart tax savings.

Evelyn is a highly respected featured commentator on radio and television programs across the nation and author of thousands of tax articles and analysis for numerous publications in print and online. In 1999, she was appointed by the Premier of Manitoba to be a Commissioner for the Lower Tax Commission.

Evelyn is also an award-winning entrepreneur, several times over, having achieved national recognition as winner of the prestigious Canadian Woman Entrepreneur of the Year Award.

Currently she sits on a number of boards including the Board of Associates at the University of Manitoba, Advisor's Edge Magazine and a provincial chapter of Advocis. She is a past member of the Public Utilities Board of Manitoba and a past executive of The Winnipeg Chamber of Commerce.